Go
a Little
Further

TORCHBEARERS
international

Royalties from the sale of this book will be donated to a sponsorship fund to provide scholarships to Torchbearer Bible Schools.

Go
a Little
Further

W. Ian Thomas
and the
Torchbearers Story

Joan Thomas

PUBLICATIONS
Fort Washington, PA 19034

Go a Little Further

Published by CLC Publications

U.S.A.
P.O. Box 1449, Fort Washington, PA 19034

UNITED KINGDOM
CLC International (UK)
51 The Dean. Alresford, Hampshire, SO24 9BJ

ISBN (paperback): 978-1-61958-176-0
ISBN (e-book): 978-1-61958-177-7

Printed in the United States of America

Table of Contents

Who "Did It?"

There is something which makes Christianity more than a religion, more than an ethic, and more than the idle dream of a sentimental idealist. It is this something which makes it relevant to each one of us right now as a contemporary experience. It is the fact that Christ *Himself* is the very life content of the Christian faith. It is He Who makes it "tick." "Faithful is He that calleth you, *Who also will do it.*" (1 Thessalonians 5:24 KJV) The One Who calls you is the One Who does that to which He calls you. "For it is God Who worketh in you, both to will and to do of His good pleasure." (Philippians 2:13 KJV). He is Himself the very dynamic of all His demands.

So begins Ian Thomas' first book, *The Saving Life of Christ*. Married for almost sixty-six years to the author of that book, I had every opportunity at close hand to observe how this, the basis for his ministry, worked out in practical, everyday experience. Frequently asked how Torchbearers came into being, all Ian would ever reply was, "God did it!" Now, under pressure from many friends who wish to know more detail than Ian would ever give, and some who may be encouraged and blessed to read the story of Torchbearers, I have accepted God's call to "put pen to paper" and by faith to "let Him do it!" I can understand Ian's reticence in giving a detailed explanation, lest anyone might think Torchbearers was simply the result of his own ambitions, abilities or personal efforts. While God's Word was a clear priority for Ian, with little time for other Christian books, he regularly read Oswald Chambers' *My Utmost for His Highest* at breakfast and insisted that the children listen quietly. Ian most certainly agreed with "Ossie" (as our children named the author), with one particular statement from the daily reading especially remembered. Oswald Chambers writes of true Christians: "We are not in God's showroom, we are here to exhibit one thing—the absolute captivity of our lives to Jesus Christ."[1]

1

The Evangelist and the Soldier

As a boy of just twelve years of age, Ian was truly captured by Jesus Christ. Reared in a fine home in London, the youngest of five children who were given every opportunity by their parents to receive a good education and to have high moral standards, they went regularly to the local Anglican church. It seems the family all had Bibles, but as Ian later admitted, "we never read them." The vicar of the church, a friend of the family, visited the home but never spoke about Christ, nor of a relationship with Him. It was a friend of Ian's, a boy of thirteen, who had become a true Christian at a Crusader camp, who first took an interest in Ian. He wanted him to come to know Christ too and so invited Ian, the year after his own experience, to spend a week with Crusaders, an organization designed to lead school boys to Christ. So, not in a church, but under the roof of a large tent, along with other boys like himself, Ian heard of a Savior, God's Son, the Lord Jesus, Who loved him and died in his place for his sins. He fully understood that he now should thank Jesus for doing so. All he could say to himself at that moment was that nobody had ever told him. Almost at once, in the quietness of his own heart and unknown to anyone, Ian quite simply received Christ and thanked Him for dying in his place so that his sins could be forgiven.

With typical enthusiasm, Ian returned home from camp and told his brothers that he had become a Christian. Their response was to call him "Bible Bill" and to throw his Bible across the table, while his concerned mother found some medication to calm young Ian's nerves!

Despite the lack of encouragement at home, Ian was able to attend further Crusader camps and activities, in particular the Sunday afternoon Bible studies where he learned much more about this "new life" and where he was later to become involved in leading the Bible classes himself. At school he was unafraid in acknowledging his new relationship with Jesus Christ. On one occasion, he was attending a class for those students of his age, who were shortly to be confirmed, as is normal in the Church of England. Ian was about fifteen years of age when he stood up in the class and addressed the teacher saying, "Excuse me, sir, but shouldn't a boy be born again before he is confirmed?" The teacher answered rather angrily, "Don't put unnecessary difficulties before the other boys."

A Hopeless Failure?

It was not long before Ian discovered that zeal and enthusiasm for this new life, which he had come to embrace so passionately, were insufficient to keep him going in God's service. In short, he had become exhausted! Perhaps the explanation for this can be no better expressed than in the last chapter of a book entitled, *They Found the Secret*, by the late Dr. Raymond Edman,

who was at that time the president of Wheaton College and who
had invited Ian to speak there. According to Dr. Edman:

> Some Christians learn that the Lord can make life an
> adventure. Major W. Ian Thomas of England is one of them.
> At the age of 15, he felt convinced that he should de-
> vote all of his life to the service of the Lord Jesus. . . . He
> began to preach, out in the open air at Hampstead Heath,
> at that early age. He was also actively engaged in Sunday
> School work, as well as in the Crusaders' Bible Class. Life
> began to be a round of ceaseless activity. . . .
> The first missionary influence in young Ian's life came
> through a doctor serving in Nigeria. . . . So it became his
> ambition to go to Nigeria and to be a doctor.
> At the university Ian became a leader in the Inter-Varsi-
> ty Fellowship group. If ever there was any evangelistic activ-
> ity going on, this youthful zealot was "buzzing around the
> place," . . . He started a slum club down in the east end of
> London. . . . "Every moment of my day was packed tight
> with 'doing things.'. . . Thus by the age of 19, I had been
> reduced to a state of complete exhaustion spiritually, until I
> felt that there was no point in going on.
> "I got down on my knees before God and I just wept
> in sheer despair. I said, 'Oh, God, I know I am saved. I
> love Jesus Christ. . . . I have tried to my uttermost to serve
> Thee but I am a hopeless failure'. . . . That night things
> happened!
> "I can honestly say I had never once heard from the
> lips of men the message that came to me . . . . but God that
> night simply focused upon me the Bible message of *Christ
> Who IS our Life*. . . . The Lord seemed to make it plain to
> me that night, through my tears of bitterness: 'You see, for
> seven years with utmost sincerity, you have been trying to
> live *for* Me, on My behalf, the life that I have been waiting
> for seven years to live *through* you.'

"That night, all in the space of an hour, I discovered the secret of the adventurous life. I got up the next morning to an entirely different Christian life but I want to emphasize this: I had not received one iota more than I already had for seven years!"

Thus step by step the Most High led His trusting, obedient servant into paths that he did not foresee nor choose, but they were pathways of service eminently satisfying and always adventurous. Instead of medical school and the mission field, the ministry was evangelism throughout Britain, especially among young people. Before World War 2 broke out, he had six wonderful years of ever-expanding ministry sharing the secret of the Life that is Christ.

Handsome and Happy

Those "six wonderful years of ever-expanding ministry" saw Ian traveling in a little two-seater Ford, with no financial support, but with ever-increasing joy and much spiritual fruit, engaged in preaching Christ wherever he was invited. His ministry took him to many church fellowships, children's missions, school groups and much more, throughout the British Isles. He also organized summer beach and sailing camps for boys. The main purpose was always to lead men, women, boys and girls to Christ that they too might discover this glorious life-changing relationship to the Lord Jesus Christ, which had become Ian's life passion. Some of the results may be found in the letters, especially those from boys and girls, in which they express their delight in attending Ian's meetings and in their simple way coming to know for themselves Christ as Savior. Files of some such letters still remain with me from as far back as the late 1930s with refreshingly clear and simple expressions of the writers' new-found life in Jesus.

From Ronald in 1936: "I am finding it hard already not to let the Lord down but I hope I will not, but instead go all the way with Him," and from Ella in Belfast: "There are five people in our house. My sister and I are the only ones saved. Would you pray for the rest of the family? I pray every night." From Nellie: "The first time I came to your meeting. That was last year, and every night from then I have asked the Lord Jesus to come into my heart and I really think he has come to stay." Doreen in Nottingham wrote: "I am 11 years of age. I have asked the Lord Jesus to come into my heart (2-28-38) Sunday. I read my Bible every day and enjoy reading it." Bill wrote: "I got your letter and I have read it over and over and I have still got Jesus in my heart." From William: "I was glad to think many more boys were saved throughout the camp and I hope they live up to it and that a little talk with Jesus will make things right, all right." (That last line is part of a favorite chorus sung by children in those days.)

There were many more such letters—simple expressions of new-found life in Christ, and there were letters from adults too.

Ian was introduced to Northern Ireland by another evangelist and good friend, Tom Rees, whose ministry in the British Isles and elsewhere was also greatly blessed. Ian had led a number of evangelistic campaigns or "missions," as they were then called, in Belfast where my family lived, although we had never met him. He was scheduled in 1938 to be the speaker at a three-week mission in a small nondenominational church hall near our home. It had been arranged earlier that Ian be hosted by our friends Mr. and Mrs. Guthrie. However, it so happened that Dr. Bingham, founder of the Sudan Interior Mission, arrived in Belfast. Having been welcomed on former occasions to the Guthrie home with the offer to stay at any future time, this now coincided with Ian's visit. The Guthries could now no longer accommodate Ian Thomas, having only one guest room in their home. It was to my ever-hospitable mother, poor widow though she was, that Mrs. Guthrie turned for help, requesting that we offer accommodation to the young, unknown evangelist from London. My mother was glad to do so. Thus, Dr. Bingham became part of the Torchbearer Story!

At the time of Ian Thomas' visit, I was enrolled in a final year of special schooling at a college across town in the hope of entering university, yet I found myself able to attend almost all Ian's evening meetings, as well as the early morning prayer sessions. On occasion and much to my surprise, Ian would escort me to a local bus stop where I found transport to college!

At the age of about seven, in the context of a loving Christian home, I had definitely and simply accepted the Lord Jesus as my personal Savior. I loved Him deeply with all my heart and cherished the ambition to become a missionary one day. Our family supported foreign missions, with missionaries and their children sometimes staying in our small and humble home. With a sign in the front window we, as children, even sold to friends and neighbors the many kittens produced by our much-loved cat, and the "profits" were given for missionary work. The Christian life kept us busy. We walked to church and Sunday school three times on the Lord's Day because it was unacceptable for Christians to use public transport on Sundays, nor were we permitted to play sports or games on Sunday. Being a Christian meant ridicule at school, and knocking on people's doors with tracts. The Christian life was serious business and a life for which I was not really sure if I was capable.

The evangelist Ian and his teaching were obviously serious business too, but the Christ Who indwelt him made him really and truly happy—even fun! He had great joy, personal and real in Jesus, the first hint to me of that kind of relationship with my Lord for which I had always longed.

The meetings came to an end, but not before this happy, handsome (I thought!) evangelist had become a family friend, had helped me on occasions with my chemistry studies, and promised to write after his return to England, saying he would send me an address list of boys and girls to whom he regularly mailed Scripture Union notes. Perhaps I would kindly add his list to a similar one of mine, which served the same purpose of encouraging newly converted boys and girls to the reading of God's Word and so to grow in Him. Ian's idea was, I discovered later, a good excuse for correspondence between us.

Despite, or maybe because of, Ian's help with my study of chemistry, I failed the examination a second time and finally decided to train as a children's nurse in preparation for whatever missionary service God might have in mind for me. My best girl friend and I had already made a plan that if neither of us should marry, we would go to Egypt and care for children in an orphanage, since we had already met missionaries from that part of the world.

Meanwhile, I felt called of God to evangelize everyone in the hospital where I had been accepted as a probationer nurse! Living in the hospital, which was necessary in those days, I found myself for the first time in my life in a world of godless people, totally disinterested in hearing about a God who loved them, or of a Savior who died to forgive their sins. I discovered the ugly side of humanity from which I had been protected in my churchgoing and in the comfortable confines of a good Christian home. I found that the feeble attempts on my part at talking about Jesus Christ to anyone in the hospital, apart from the sick little children for whom I loved to care, were greeted with absolute disdain or at least, amusement. Now *I* was the "total failure."

My answer came out of desperation when I rose very early one morning, and calling on God, I asked for help and read His Word. I was struggling through Second Corinthians, particularly, "thanks be unto God, which always causeth us to triumph *in Christ*" (2:14, KJV, emphasis added). I told God that was not true—at least not in my case—until on rereading the verse, I saw that apart from depending by faith on Christ, whose life I had received when I was born again, there could never be any expectation of ministering Christ to others. Years later, Ian was to describe what this discovery meant in words now familiar to many Christians:

> I can't, HE never said I could,
> But HE can, and always said HE would.
> Then you can truly say, "HE did it"!

From Mission Field to Battlefield

After the mission meetings in Belfast, the first letter from Ian with his promised list of addresses of boys and girls arrived in the mail at our home. It did occur to me that for him to mail this list from England to Ireland and for me to mail the notes back to those addresses in England was just a little unnecessary, even extravagant. However, I did what I was told even as I would be doing in days to come. I wrote a "Dear Mr. Thomas" reply to say I had received his letter with the list, but promptly I received a letter back thanking me for mine! Letters came and letters went, as it was to be throughout our lives. Long before the discovery of e-mail, only our all-wise, wonderful God must have known that Ian and I would need further practice in writing letters, as Torchbearers developed around the world.

Ian came to speak at meetings in other parts of Belfast on two more occasions. He visited at our home, but he did not stay with us since our "friendship" was kept very secret from all others, except my understanding mother.

War changes things, and so it was in September, 1939. Ian had had army training in the OTC at high school and having been commissioned already as an officer in the Royal Fusiliers, he was now recalled to that regiment immediately at the outbreak of World War II. The Royal Fusiliers is an infantry regiment—in fact it is officially the "City of London Regiment," with its headquarters in the Tower of London, all of which made Ian justly proud, being himself a Londoner. As "2nd Lieutenant Ian Thomas," he was dispatched with his regiment in 1940 to face the early fighting in France and Belgium. Even from the "war zone," I received letters. One of these mentioned a letter sent to Ian by my mother in which she included "a little sermonette which was greatly appreciated as I have not heard one Christian sermon since I have been in France and have not yet met one single Christian. You may imagine that even 'potted sermons' in pen and ink are like water in a dry land." Ian then wrote, "I do thank God for the many dear saints who are constantly praying for me and it makes me feel utterly unworthy! I have had over 60 letters in the last two weeks and quite a number, thank God, from those who have been converted during evangelistic meetings and campaigns. That always thrills me immensely!" He went on, "Don't imagine now that you need not write any more. There are none that I look forward to more than yours! I pray for you too, for all His will to be worked out in you to His own eternal glory." Although I hardly believed my letters were so important, I got the message.

Those readers familiar with the course of World War II will remember that in May 1940, the fighting in France and Belgium culminated in the evacuation of many thousands of British and French troops under constant enemy fire from the beaches at Dunkirk across the English Channel and back to Britain. Sadly, many were left behind, wounded, killed, captured or missing. After Dunkirk, in a letter from Ian on his safe return to England, he wrote, "Hallelujah for a mighty deliverance and for a very deep sense of His continual presence throughout."

His now-familiar letters continued to arrive even more frequently, this time to the door of the hospital in Belfast where I was in training. Following his return from France, Ian was stationed with his regiment in England. It was moved to different parts of the country so that invariably he found fellowship in places where he had ministered as an evangelist in prewar days and was happy when churches where he had formerly preached invited him to speak. Fellow army officers were sometimes mystified that Ian could always find friends wherever the regiment was stationed. Later, during the North African campaign, they were more amazed that he contacted "friends" even in the desert—two elderly lady missionaries whom he had known before World War II in England!

Ian was now able to visit Belfast on occasion when on leave, even when I had no leave from the hospital. Plus, his letters continued to arrive. One day the postman brought a very particular and unexpected letter, in which Ian asked the famous question, "Will you marry me?" It certainly took a long sleepless and prayerful night for me to write back the answer, "Yes!"

Then the day came when at the front door of the small hospital where I lived and worked, and within which nurses were neither permitted to receive nor entertain visitors, Ian came one rainy evening and placed a small diamond ring on my finger. Far too soon he had to hurry away to preach, and I needed to report for night duty. The situation was hardly romantic—but certainly most memorable. I think God smiled, and in His heart, only to Himself, may have whispered "Torchbearers"!

Warnings, Wedding and War

Following our engagement, Ian was able to visit Belfast on only a few occasions. As the war continued to spread quickly in Europe and then to North Africa, he gave me definite warning that he could be called at any time for overseas military duty for possibly two years or more. We mutually agreed to be married before his possible departure with his regiment.

I received another warning before our wedding. Although very personal, I feel it needs to be written so that family, friends, staff, and those who are happy to call themselves Torchbearers, can better understand the strong conviction and call of God that Ian accept literally what the Lord Jesus meant when He said in Matthew 10:38, "Anyone who does not take his cross and follow me is not worthy of me" (NIV 1984), and in John 12:24, "unless a grain of wheat falls into the earth and dies, it remains by itself alone; but if it dies, it bears much fruit" (NASB).

Recently I found the following lines tucked away with some of Ian's papers, titled "Consecration."

> Be gone each earthborn tie and bond
> Be gone affection deep and fond,
> Which Christ doth not partake;
> Have I a box of alabaster
> That is not broken for my Master
> To which my heart still clings the faster
> Help me my box to break.

Upon my callous heart impress,
The height and depth of all Thy grace,
That I may love Thee more;
That Thou canst find in me Thy pleasure,
That Thou canst call a worm Thy treasure
Tells of a love I cannot measure,
But worship and adore.

Ian wrote the following words to me in a letter before we were married, and I keep the original on my desk:

You will understand me fully, I know Joan, when I say that you can never have more than second place in my life, for the first place has been eternally reserved for the Savior Himself. I could never be happy if I were not equally sure that I can only have second place in yours for the very same reason. But this very fact is the greatest possible guarantee that our lives shall be united in perfect happiness, for just as He is the common focus of our love, Whom above all we both seek to please, so shall our longings and all our ambitions be bound together in Him. I suppose it is hardly necessary to say that my greatest longing, the moment this war is over, is to return at once to the work to which I have been called, a work which must be accomplished with all the passion of my soul and with all the energy and devotion I can muster. Now . . . will you tell me quite frankly when you write whether this too is your greatest longing and will you tell me really right from the bottom of your own heart what your feelings are in regard to the rather nomadic life of an evangelist? Thrilling and wonderful as such a life is, there are comforts, little luxuries and the many benefits of an unbroken "home life" that have to be foregone—what would you think of that? Suppose the dear loving Lord should ask us once again, at the end of this war, to trust Him solely for the daily needs of life, as He once asked me 6 $^1/_2$ years ago—what would *your* answer be—your *real* answer, forgetting me?

For me the questions were not unexpected. Little as I knew at that time of Ian's lifestyle, his love for and total obedience to Christ in everything he did and said were absolutely obvious. However, Ian did not realize that I had seen in my home from childhood days that God and His work came before all else. We hosted preachers, missionaries, our Sunday school teachers and many others. Frequently we gave up our beds to sleep on the floor so that others could be more comfortable. As far as trusting Him solely for the daily needs of life goes, I had observed that from the age of twelve, when my beloved father died at forty-eight of a heart attack, bankrupt. My own mother, left with four children, I being the youngest, showed us what it really meant to "trust our heavenly Father solely for the daily needs of life." She did trust Him without complaints, and she kept us happy, healthy and even educated. Many years later, after my mother had been called "home," one of my sisters found in her writing case a well underlined little verse:

> "God, give me sympathy, and common sense
> And help me keep my courage high;
> God, give me calm and confidence,
> And – please – a twinkle in my eye."
> (Margaret Bailey)

Back to the wedding. Embarkation leave was short and came very quickly for Ian, but he was able to get a flight to Ireland. There was little time for preparation, so after a simple service and a two-day honeymoon, we said goodbye. However, much to Ian's surprise, when he returned to his battalion in England, he learned they were to remain possibly for another year in the British Isles. The idea that the regiment was to face the enemy, now fighting in Russia, had been pure camouflage to keep that enemy guessing. For us, it appeared we had married under false pretenses. Ian's parents kindly invited me to live with them in London so that, as far as possible, we were able to be with each other at least for short visits as Army service allowed, in some parts of England and Scotland, or wherever Ian would be stationed, and where again there were opportunities for him to minister in local churches. God always does more than we ask or think—so the honeymoon of two days extended to fifteen months.

The final and heartrending day of farewell came at a bleak railway station in Nottingham where, along with many other soldiers with wives and families, we bid goodbye—not yet knowing where the men were being sent, nor for how long. Even if they did know to which war zone they were being assigned, soldiers at that time in war were not allowed to communicate those facts to anyone. However, I guessed where Ian was when he wrote from overseas in his first letter, "The sun is scorching hot. I am writing in a shell-wrecked farm with plenty of the impediments of war lying about. The dust is incredible and all that we used to hear about the weather holding up operations, I have found to be 200 percent true. A few days ago we had a spell of tremendous wind—I have never felt anything like it but now it is really hot." This, I guessed rightly, was North Africa. Despite those conditions, Ian wrote, "Well, I got the old Book out this morning and found great comfort in Isaiah 12, especially verse 2. Read it and rest on it! I know you won't worry—all must be well for He reigns and He makes even the wrath of man to praise Him! Hallelujah! It's grand to be saved!"

In a later letter, he wrote, "Had a grand meeting for the troops a week ago and a Naval Petty Officer was saved. He had become interested through attending a French class held by one of the two lady missionaries I met.

At the end of another letter Ian said, "I'm looking forward so much to sitting around the fire with you all again; war is a ghastly business and we must all do our bit to finish it victoriously as soon as possible."

In August of 1943, Ian was in North Africa, and he mentioned having three days of rest, being "much refreshed in spirit and filled with a deepened desire to live wholly and utterly for the Lord Jesus. I have seen more clearly than ever the complete emptiness of life apart from the single purpose of bringing men, women and children to Christ—a purpose around which every other activity and circumstance must revolve. Hallelujah! What a Savior! We must pray more earnestly than ever that all His rich purposes for post-war days be brought to pass without any hindrance. Especially must we pray that everyone who forms part of the pattern may be brought of their own initiative into the scheme of things; i.e., the impulse must be from above—One Spirit directing all our ways independently into one purpose, thereby setting the seal of God upon our efforts." (Maybe God whispered to Himself again—"Torchbearer" Centres, Bible Schools.)

He Always Carried His Bible

Ian's military service in North Africa was relatively short and appeared to consist of bringing to the brigade headquarters very many disillusioned Italian soldiers awaiting the safety of becoming prisoners. In one letter he wrote, "I interrogated a prisoner yesterday who had been lying out wounded for six days without food or water. He had been warned we would ill-treat and shoot him, and he was in tears at the fair treatment he was receiving. It was very sad to see the snaps [photos] of his two kiddies."

Before leaving North Africa, Ian had seven days leave and was grateful for the opportunity to travel with a convoy going to Jerusalem. He wrote, "Within two hours of my arrival, I was giving my testimony at a Christian Fellowship Meeting." He was able to bathe in the Sea of Galilee, visit Bethlehem, the garden tomb, and much more, and to end the experience by saying, "Praise the Lord for the wonderful opportunity to see the Land of the Book."

It was not long before Ian's address changed so that he was allowed to tell me that he was in Italy, and that "for the hot sun in the desert we now have mud, snow and cold." He said that though he was only thirty to forty yards from the enemy at the time of writing, there was nothing for me to worry about because he knew that "your trust is in God and we are agreed that our times are in His hands." Very soon another letter came in which Ian asked me to thank friends who were praying for him "which I value more than I can say. One needs to hold fast to the promises! Not a hair of the head . . . and Psalm 91 . . . and above all to trust that one does not get barren or stale. It is very difficult in this awful atmosphere to remember that the whole purpose of living is to bring others to the knowledge of 'Life which is more abundant.'" Then Ian added: "The destruction here is beyond description—the tide of war moves so slowly in this mountainous type of country that nothing escapes the battle zones. However, praise God, beyond it all, we know the Day must dawn when tears and sighing will be banished and Christ Himself shall reign in righteousness."

Since back home in England we were able to hear continually on our radios—no TV in those days—the course of World War II, I was not surprised to learn from Ian that with allied troops from the USA, New Zealand, Australia, India and elsewhere, his Regiment had been involved in the fourth and finally successful, but terrible, battle at Monte Cassino in May of 1944. I think Ian's personal part in this can best be described by a fellow company commander in his memoirs that were written and printed in England many years later: "At first light on the 18th, Ian Thomas climbed up to the monastery with his batman Fusilier Barden. Just short of the monastery, they found twenty Germans in a cave, who surrendered, waving a 'white' tablecloth taken from the monastery. Major Thomas went into the monastery, arriving just after two Polish officers who officially were to take the surrender of Germans at the monastery. He collected the Polish officers' signatures on the flyleaf of his Bible which he always carried! He also collected a few charred picture postcards before returning to us. The tablecloth is now in the Royal Fusiliers Museum in the Tower of London."

Unfortunately, that Bible got lost or possibly stolen shortly after this time.

Ian mailed the old torn tablecloth back to me, however, including the Italian soil left falling out of it, and having sent it to the Museum, I took the opportunity when happening to be in London with some friends to view the exhibition. There was a small fee to be paid—and there still is—but when I explained I was Major Thomas' wife and wished to see "his tablecloth," I was told I need not pay. Then the colonel was brought from the nearby headquarters to meet me. He was pleased to discuss Ian's part in the regiment's successes, and then posed the question: "Didn't you people take 'holy orders' or something?" I attempted a suitable reply, but regret that I did not have the courage to tell the colonel that ever since we came to know Christ, we had always sought to do so.

After Cassino, some men were given varying spells of leave and were sent to a rest area to reinforce and reorganize. Ian wrote: "Here I am, straight from the horrors of the Cassino battle, in the sunshine, a few yards from the sea—it seems incredible. Only one Person could have brought me through unharmed and if He did that, it has been laid upon my heart more powerfully than ever these last few days that it must only be that my life, linked with yours, shall be utterly poured out for Christ and the salvation of precious souls. I found a small Waldensian church here where a grand Christian fellowship has sprung up among service men and I had a wonderful Sunday, with two faithful messages. Then on Monday evening, there was a Fellowship and Testimony meeting, at the end of which I spoke and the power of God was mighty. One lad was definitely saved, another gained assurance, and all of us were blessed. Hallelujah!"

The time of "rest" was over all too soon, as the Allies moved north from Monte Cassino. At a later battle, a shell fired at Ian's company from an enemy Tiger tank hit and removed one of his fingers so that he had to go to a field hospital for treatment. Sadly two other men nearby were killed because of the same shell, and two others wounded. The surgeon was able to keep the knuckle joint on Ian's finger intact, so that it remained partly useful, even as a sermon illustration. Ian would say, "I could have a rubber dummy fixed in the place of the missing one to look just like a real finger, and I would not mind even if you stepped on it because I would not feel any pain. There are people who sit in church, looking like believers, but if they have never truly come to receive life in Christ, they would simply be like my dummy finger, but spiritually lifeless." That was a good illustration, but a painful one, especially as Ian needed to have a further operation when the finger became infected.

There was increasing military action as the Allies moved further into the north of Italy. At one time several of Ian's senior officers, including the colonel, were wounded, but Ian only sustained minor wounds to his face, so he admitted to being grateful to God that by His goodness, God had allowed him to fulfill one of his earthly ambitions to bear the title of lieutenant colonel and to be in command of the whole Battalion! Of course this was only a temporary appointment until the colonel would return, recovered from his wounds. I had to admit that I was proud to write my next letters for about three weeks to Lieutenant Colonel W. Ian Thomas. When the colonel returned for duty, Ian once again reverted to major, but with the arrangement that he would never carry a rank below major and could retain that title in civilian life.

Far more exciting for me was to hear from Ian that his leave, after almost two years overseas, was to occur soon. While we sorrowed greatly for the families of those whose loved ones would never come home, many of whom we knew personally, yet we could believe that almighty God had plans unknown to us at the time but most certainly for His glory.

2

A Large House Somewhere

For those wives whose husbands have served in wars overseas, or for parents of missionaries whose sons or daughters have spent many years away from home, you will know the sheer joy of first of all anticipating their return, and then experiencing the reality. Ian wrote a "crazy" (as he called it) letter in January of 1945 to say that he had just heard a secret, which I should keep to myself, that he would be coming home on leave. He wrote, "Needless to say, when I heard the news I said Hallelujah 75 times in quick succession and shouted glory till the filament in the electric light bulb broke!"

However, peace in Europe was not signed until May of 1945, and the anticipation of his return lasted until July, and even then, he only had five weeks of leave. However, the reality was, as anyone knows who has experienced a long separation following the awful dangers of war, a moment never to be forgotten of extreme joy and happiness, mingled with deepest gratitude to almighty God.

Ian was to meet his small son, Christopher, whom he had never seen. Both had viewed each other's framed photograph, so Ian wrote ahead of time, "Try your hardest to convince young Christopher that his father's face does not really feel like a piece of glass—nor is it usually kept in a frame, wooden or otherwise. I should hate to find him clinging to a picture on the wall, whilst rejecting his legitimate father!"

Ian was also to stay in a house he owned but had never seen. I had already been living there with my mother and young Christopher, Ian having arranged for me to pay for it in installments, which I withdrew from his military earnings in the bank. While he was overseas, I had been living in Nottingham with a very good friend whose husband was involved in war service away from home, but I desperately needed to find a house where my mother could be with me when the baby would arrive. Available houses were extremely difficult to find in war time, and any vacant ones were immediately filled by the authorities with soldiers, or refugees from bombed cities.

By one of those incredible ways which can be explained only in terms of God's intervention, I did hear about the possibility of such a house, but was told that the owner was so bad tempered no one could even approach her. To that, my Irish spirit rose up within me. In answer to my knock on her door, the lady opened an inch and demanded, "Where is your husband?" Hearing he had just been involved with his regiment in military service in Greece before being sent to Italy, she shouted, "Come in." I soon discovered that this widowed lady appeared to have cherished some unusually happy memories of a vacation in Greece, shared in the past with her now-deceased husband. Asking me various questions about Ian's impressions of Greece, I assured her that he had appreciated the kindness and friendliness of the people.

Seeing her obvious and unexpected interest, I added a few more details as best as I could remember, along with other facts which I felt would be honest and appropriate. Suddenly the "bad-tempered lady" asked me if I had come to see her concerning the house which she owned higher up the road. If so, she would sell for six hundred English pounds. I replied that I thought we could manage that amount.

When Ian finally returned home on leave, I was proud to introduce him to our handsome little son, now happily settled in his dad's new home—my bargain house. A semi-detached three-story brick house, it had three bedrooms, a bathroom, an attic on the third floor—which could be made into a small bedroom—two living rooms downstairs and a kitchen. At the front entrance there was even a tiny garden—or rather a few square inches of unmown grass. Since Ian and I had never had the opportunity to "set up home," it was a help that when my mother came to live with me, she came along with her furniture.

Soon after, Ian arrived, delighted with his house. I was amused to find that having decided the old staircase should be painted, he found his way to town and bought paint, the color of which displayed on the tin was "Battleship Grey!" He quickly went to work, quite alone, on the simple task which seemed, I observed, to be a kind of therapy after the many months of war which he had so recently experienced. No psychiatrist required for this soldier.

During the following summer while Ian was at home again, he was invited by his good friend, the evangelist Tom Rees, to speak for a week at Hildenborough Hall—a magnificent country mansion in the south of England. Tom had recently purchased it, making it into a "Christian Holiday Conference Center." I believe that Tom, having ministered in the United States before the war, had discovered the spiritual effectiveness of this type of ministry by introducing people of all ages to the claims of Jesus Christ in the context of a well-organized vacation program, along with Bible teaching morning and evening. This was a new concept to British Christians, who enjoyed it and were blessed, even as we were also blessed.

Ian's leave was about to end, and he would be returning to Germany all too soon with what he jokingly called "The most famous regiment in the British Army—the Royal Fusiliers." They would be a very small part of the "Army of Occupation" in Germany for some months. Known only to God Himself, there would be laid in the city of Velbert in the Rhineland a firm foundation for what in German was to be called "Die Fackelträger"— "Torchbearers."

Before leaving Nottingham and our "new" house with its freshly painted battleship-grey staircase, Ian discussed his future in God's service with me. Knowing full well that his deepest longing was most surely to return to his former traveling evangelistic ministry, I simply and clearly stated that I would expect and want him to continue as he had done before the war; and I would remain happily here in the home, or look for a simple little cottage somewhere in the country and care for the family. To my surprise, Ian said some now truly very famous words, "I think we need a large house somewhere so that we can have lots of young people to stay and teach them the truth about the Christian life." Somewhat surprised, I asked where it should be, but Ian had no answer. I produced a map of England, noting that Tom Rees already had his large house in the south of the country, so we ought not to be a rival and should look in the north. End of conversation. I admit, however, to being disinterested in any large house anywhere. I was already planning my "cottage in the country" with roses round the door and chickens happily laying their eggs for us in a small outhouse with an open door—those "free-range" eggs, so good for the kids.

Nothing further was discussed between us about "a large house somewhere," and we were about to experience almost another year of separation in which God would write what would be to us a new part of His story.

The Army of Occupation

To many Christians seeking God's will in their lives, the words from Proverbs 16:9 often ring true: "The heart of man plans his way, but the LORD establishes his steps." Ian's plan to return to his earlier evangelistic traveling ministry was indeed to be continued, but in a very different way. Though delayed in his plans by becoming part of the Army of Occupation in Germany, this would be crucial to the foundation of The Capernwray Missionary Fellowship of Torchbearers.

Ian arrived in the town of Velbert, situated in the British zone of North Germany, where he first had the task of obtaining accommodations for those many military personnel who were to be stationed in that particular area. The local authorities provided him with two lists of names and addresses of possible locations. The first consisted of the private homes of local citizens and the second list, of various factories and business facilities. To announce to German families that they must leave their own homes and to owners of businesses that they must evacuate their premises to provide housing for former enemies, was no easy, nor pleasant, assignment. I did not wonder that Ian wrote to ask me to pray that in doing so he might not cause too much difficulty or inconvenience for the people concerned.

One of the initial homes he chose was at 84 Hindenburg-strasse where he found the Witte family, which included mother, dad, and three delightful blonde-haired children. On hearing from Ian that they must leave their home, Hans Witte explained that in anticipation of such a possibility he had already kept a room available in his factory, situated within the town.

Eberhard, the son of the family, was the last to leave the house, so Ian was extra kind and sent him off with a few chocolates and a note of greeting to the family. In it he mentioned that his mother would be welcome to return to the home at any time to take care of the flowers and plants which grew in the conservatory attached to the house.

Imagine the joy Ian had on receiving a letter from Hans Witte written in English and in neat handwriting. I continue to cherish the original greatly, which reads:

> Dear Mr. Thomas,
>
> After leaving our house last Saturday with tears and a very heavy heart, as we told you, we had two kind moments yesterday.
>
> At first your greetings through our son brought light in our new home. Many thanks for it.
>
> As second we heard that we are bound with one another through Jesus Christ.
>
> With very kind regards, also from my wife and the children,
>
> Yours very sincerely, Hans Witte

With his deepest gratitude to our wonderful Lord, Ian could see that God's good hand was even on this time of seeming delay to his "deepest longing to return to the work to which he had been called." Here were believers—members with us, their former enemies, of the same family—the worldwide church of Jesus Christ, our Savior and Lord. In the coming days we were to keep in close touch with the Witte family and on later visits to Germany, there was always the most genuine and warmest welcome for us to stay at their home.

Ian was to come to know other believers and their families in the town of Velbert during the year in which he served in the Army of Occupation. He was invited to preach in their churches, to meet families and friends in their homes, and in future days on many occasions, to preach and teach God's Word throughout Germany.

While in Velbert, Ian joined a small group of British military personnel who, as Christians, began to gather regularly in the town for the purpose of sharing times of fellowship, prayer and Bible study. Among them was a military nurse. Brenda had come to Christ before the war when Ian held evangelistic meetings in Bolton, her hometown in the north of England. Later on, she was to join with us in the ministry that still lay ahead in England, as did Gordon, a Royal Fusilier who shared in the group and became a true friend and colleague.

That God frequently uses small things, casual "happenings" and ordinary people to accomplish His bigger purposes is obvious, not only as recorded in God's Word for our encouragement, but in the experience of many of us. So it was during Ian's year of military service in the occupation of Germany. This time the "small thing," I think, was simply an ordinary British magazine, which had likely been sent to some soldier who left it just "lying around somewhere" and which Ian "happened" to find. This magazine usually included pictures of large and expensive houses which were for sale in England at the time. Due to the unavoidable neglect of such property during the war years, those who owned these homes now found they could no longer afford to maintain such large buildings and estates, nor were they able to find, nor pay the cost of hiring, the many servants required for the upkeep of such grand houses. As Ian, quite casually, turned the pages, his attention was drawn to one estate in particular with the curious name of "Capernwray Hall." Could this possibly be that "large house somewhere" about which we had talked in our own little home in Nottingham just about a year ago? Could we have "lots of young people" stay there? It appeared in the magazine almost like a castle with its tower and mock stone battlements above the seemingly ancient walls. It looked big enough, strong enough—and no doubt with foundations good enough—if it was to be filled with lots of British young people!

Better still, Capernwray Hall was situated, not just "somewhere" but in the *north* of England, close to the beautiful Lake District and within an hour's bus ride of the Scottish border.

I was soon to hear further details—and to receive my instructions.

The Big House

The postman did indeed bring me those instructions very soon from Germany. Ian had discovered that Capernwray Hall was to be sold at auction in the town hall of Lancaster on the 11th of September 1946, "at 1 p.m. (promptly)"according to the large brochure which the postman delivered to me. The building was but part of "the freehold, agricultural sporting property known as 'Capernwray Hall Estate' comprising Capernwray Hall and Borwick Hall with 12 valuable farms, small holdings, cottages, small saw mill, well timbered woodlands, small sporting properties and fishing rights."

On turning the pages of the auctioneer's brochure, I was relieved to find that the twelve farms and other parts of the estate were to be sold separately to other prospective buyers. Capernwray Hall itself was described as "The attractive and very substantially built country mansion of *medium* size." At the same time, along with the main house, there were three cottages, fifty-four acres of land, a small lake, and a private church with seating for sixty-eight persons, all included with Capernwray Hall and to be sold together at the auction.

Ian instructed me from Germany that, as he was unable to obtain leave from the army either to see the building or to attend the auction himself, that I should do so in his place. I had never even attended an auction! He suggested that I ask his good friend, Doug Stocken, a Christian businessman in Nottingham, to accompany me and to take care of the bidding. Ian stated a figure beyond which we should not go, since he had calculated that it might just be sufficient for a down payment on the property and that he had very little money left in his pocket after that. Doug was no more enthusiastic than I, but we were both willing to obey Ian's instructions and, for myself, I knew there were God's clear instructions in His Word concerning "obeying your husband in the Lord."

The day before the auction, I was happy to have the company of Doug and his wife as he drove us in his Jaguar (the highlight of my day) to Carnforth, the town four miles from Capernwray Hall. We found accommodation for a night's stay in a village nearer to the Hall, then Doug, strolling in the small main street before turning in for the night, unexpectedly met the auctioneer who was to be responsible for the sale of the estate the following day. On hearing that Doug had come to attend the auction for Capernwray Hall itself and having been told the purpose for our doing so, the auctioneer responded, "I will do my best for you and there will be a seat for you at the front!"

Since we were required to attend the auction at the town hall "at 1 p.m. promptly," we arrived as soon as it was possible after breakfast, ready to view this "medium-sized mansion." We soon discovered that a small part of the building dated all the way back to the 1600s and that the Marton family had owned the home for a number of generations. However, there had been some sixty children living in the Hall during the war years. They were from a church boarding school in Lancaster mainly intended for orphaned children, and they had been evacuated to Capernwray in the possible event of the city being hit in an air raid. Since the war had ended, the children had returned to Lancaster, leaving the house empty and ready to be sold. A remaining relative of the Marton family, few of whom were still alive, would benefit from the sale.

The headmaster of the school, Rev. Edmonds, and his wife were still in residence, and it was Mrs. Edmonds who would take us on a tour of the building, which I quickly assessed not "of medium size" at all, but huge. Advertised as having twenty-four bedrooms (with only four bathrooms), there were obviously many more small rooms for housekeepers, cooks and other servants. There was accommodation for, we were told, seven gardeners, groomsmen for the care of the horses, and a whole "nursery wing" that the Marton's children and their nannies had used for several generations.

We entered Capernwray Hall by a massive carved oak door, then through the "lofty and spacious hall" to the library (41 by 24 ft.), on to the dining room (36 by 24 ft.), a "drawing room"—or as it was originally named a "with-drawing room"—(34 by 18 ft.), then a "billiard room" (28 x 17 ft.), and then to "the study" (17 by 15 ft.) which, the brochure stated, was "fitted with very interesting old oak paneling." The kitchen was enormous as well, and I noted that against one wall stood a long line of very small wash basins for the school children, while in one of the storerooms two cold showers were available. Mrs. Edmonds led us out to the large courtyard with its cobblestones and a clock tower, which had partly fallen into disrepair. We viewed the "stabling for 11 horses," but I was not so sure there was space for "garages for 5 cars."

This was indeed a well-built and attractive "big house somewhere" with room for "lots of young people." Never farmed, the grounds were extensive, though neglected, and there were indeed some "stately forest trees" in the parkland. The large "kitchen garden" could maybe produce vegetables and possibly a farm be established so that cattle and sheep could graze if the pasture were developed. We did notice that at some time tennis had been played on the old grass court, but if the place were to become a "Christian Holiday Conference Center" for young people, many other outdoor activities would need to be planned as well. The "sunken garden" with its lily pond and rose beds must have been most attractive at some time in the past, but now it was largely overgrown, apart from a couple of small rose-bushes that remained visible amidst the weeds.

What about the inside of the house itself? Bunk beds? More bathrooms? Kitchen equipment? Heating and water supply? Alterations to houses were not permitted by the authorities following the war, as priority was given to restoring essential facilities, such as schools, hospitals and government buildings, which had been lost or damaged in war time. As I walked along the cold, flagstone corridors downstairs with their high ceilings, then stood in the massive empty rooms, many uncertain thoughts filled my mind. Nevertheless, viewing the fine building from the outside with its huge and welcoming oak door, then turning to see the truly extensive view of grassy hillsides, and the tiny "peek" of England's beautiful Lake District, somehow my thoughts changed.

"Why are you interested in Capernwray Hall at a time like this, so soon after the war?" Mrs. Edmonds asked. When she heard that the possibility was for the establishment of a Christian youth center, she replied, "Then I hope very much that you will be successful with your bid at the auction." When I said that I assumed not many people had shown interest in the Hall, Mrs. Edmonds told me otherwise.

It was almost time to leave that "big house," and we would know very soon if our bid was to be successful. In my heart, I was blessed and assured to know that God Himself already knew exactly what His plans were, and that He would direct our thoughts as we kept our trust securely in Him. Surely, once again God would "do it" as He had demonstrated in the past.

Just Go a Little Further

In the summer of 1946, when we spoke of the "big house" where we could have "lots of young people to stay," Ian could not have known that he would be back in Germany when God would reveal His choice. He could not have known that he would need to send me in his stead since he could not get leave to view Capernwray Hall or to bid at the auction. In any case, God knew that perhaps Ian's bid might have been different from mine.

Doug Stocken and I arrived at the Lancaster Town Hall to find that many interested people and prospective bidders were already seated. We had been told that Colonel George Marton, the last member of his family to own the estate, was in the habit of riding regularly on horseback to his farms and properties in order to collect, for himself, the regular amount of rent owed by his tenants. Now, at the auction there was the opportunity for those tenants to purchase their farms for themselves if at all possible. Many of these were attending the auction, in addition to those interested in nearby "Borwick Hall," which was included in Col. Marton's large estate. This was a much older building than Capernwray, where "Bonnie Prince Charlie" was reputed to have stayed overnight as he fled from the English back home to Scotland.

We took our seats in the front row of the Lancaster Town Hall, and the bidding started with the sale of Capernwray Hall. Slowly the auctioneer took the offers, raising them by small amounts, until finally the figure was reached beyond Doug's instructions to go no further. When that time came, he turned to me and whispered, "What shall I do?" With little hesitation and hardly realizing the importance of my whisper, I replied, "Just go a little further!" That turned out to be the last bid!

I was called by the auctioneer to go forward and sign my name for Capernwray Hall with its vast number of huge, empty rooms, three cottages, private church, big courtyard with its horse stables, and the surrounding acres of neglected land. We left the building as soon as possible while the rest of the Marton estate was sold.

On reaching the outside of the main door of the town hall, I leaned against the nearby wall, hardly knowing what to think except—"What *have* we done? We are crazy! We have overspent, there is no organization, no mission, no committee, no church to support us, and what a building!" I complained to God, to myself, to Doug, and to his wife most of the way home—and wondered what Ian would say upon hearing the news.

My mother welcomed me to what seemed then to be our *very small* house. After she heard we had been successful with our bid, she inquired where exactly the Hall was situated. I explained about its closeness to the Lake District, at which she exclaimed, "Of course it will be all right. Wonderful! Don't worry." Some years later, I discovered this positive attitude came about because in her girlhood days, her father owned a rarity for that time and place, one of the early Ford cars and, as an only child, my mother would be driven from her home in Liverpool to spend vacations with relatives in the Lake District. It was there that her godly grandfather spent time hiking the Lake District hills and rowing with my mother, talking frequently about his love for God, the Creator of such surrounding beauty, and about the Lord Jesus who loved her. Never having heard these truths at home, my mother connected the joys of her many visits to the Lake District with a faithful God Whom she would, herself, come to know later in life. Now she was to move with me to Capernwray Hall. There she constantly delighted, not simply in the countryside, but in meeting young people from around the world who were finding Christ, many of whom left the "big house" to share Him with friends and relatives.

But something even better was to come. As I sought direction in God's Word before I'd left home the day before the auction, I had read Psalm 31. Nothing at that time seemed to apply to the situation. Afterwards, however, I decided I should re-read that particular Psalm lest we had mistaken God's instructions by my whisper to Doug to "go a little further." Verse 8 of Psalm 31, at least in the King James Version, assured me, "Thou hast set my feet in a large room" (God Himself had done so!). In verse 19, God had His ready-made plans: "How great is thy goodness, which thou hast laid up for them that fear thee; which thou hast wrought for them that trust in thee before the sons of men!" I thought of the large library at Capernwray Hall with those rows of empty bookshelves from floor almost to ceiling, now waiting to be filled. God seemed to be saying that He was about to unfold His story.

The last verse of Psalm 31 most surely needed to be read, "Be of good courage." This instruction from an all-knowing God came with a promise, "He shall strengthen your heart, all you who hope in the Lord." I was ready for the journey.

A telegram was dispatched with the news to Ian in Germany, who said he was delighted, despite that "little bit further." I wrote these exact words in my old diary of 1946: "Wednesday 11th September. Mother's birthday. Auction. Bought Capernwray Hall £7,350." That looked like quite a present for my mother's sixtieth birthday! And more than sixty years ago, those were a lot of British pounds, of which we had to give one tenth at the time, God enabling us to pay the remainder over the following years.

I made the next entry of importance in my 1946 diary on Tuesday, November 5th: "Arrived Longlands Hotel, Tewitfield. 1:15 p.m. saw C. Hall in afternoon." Tewitfield is a tiny hamlet (even smaller than a village) and about two miles from Capernwray Hall. Not owning a car and having arrived by train at Carnforth, I had no means of transport to the Hall. Mother, my eldest sister and I were glad to find a taxi to drive us to Capernwray where we enjoyed a very quick visit to the "large house."

In retrospect, the simple entry in my diary for the following day reads as if the occasion of taking up residence in an ancient and very big, castle-like building situated in what seemed then to be "the back of beyond," was simply an everyday occurrence, and this by three women and one three-year-old boy. "November 6th. Furniture all in by 4 p.m. and we comfortably settled by evening."

Some discomfort was to come later.

3

Capernwray Hall

Waking up to very different surroundings from those of the small terrace house in which I had been living in Nottingham, it was a real delight to look out from Capernwray's huge windows to view the lush, green grass of the old croquet lawn. Behind that were massive oak, beech and chestnut trees, some turning to the golden shades of autumn. I felt I was breathing in the freshness of the English countryside. As a child living in a tiny house in the city, I had longed to spend my life in the unspoiled world of God's creative genius—this was it!

To add to my joy on that first morning of life at Capernwray Hall, a message reached me that Ian was on his way from Germany on special leave for a couple of days for the sole purpose of viewing his newly acquired "big house." He arrived about 5:00 p.m. on that very day and tried to enter by the many possible entrances, which were mostly locked. When he finally shouted loud enough for one of us to hear, he was officially welcomed to what I called "your wee home in the country." Ian hardly took time for a welcoming hug, let alone a quick cup of tea, before the two of us were off, excitedly exploring the inside of the whole building. We went from the impressive main entrance and "lounge hall" to the huge library, the dining room and drawing room, along the wide-tiled corridor, into the fine billiard room at the end of which was a door leading to what had been described as the "smoking room" with its oak paneling covering the walls. Here, Colonel Marton and his friends, after their game of billiards, would drink, smoke their pipes, and no doubt discuss their common interests.

The kitchen, which was enormous, came next with a massive table still in place in the center. Then, along the old stone-flagged corridors, there were smaller "pantries," dishwashing facilities and cleaning stores. We strode over the uncarpeted corridors upstairs and inspected all of the bedrooms, the main ones being very large, with others somewhat smaller. We also noted the really tiny rooms in the servants' quarters.

Ian mounted the many stairs taking him to the main tower where he saw that there were once bedrooms leading off from the stairway. We later learned that during the Marton family's residence, there had been a fire in the tower which burned all but the stone staircase and the walls of the tower itself. Ian decided then and there that the rooms could be rebuilt, and he could use the top room for his office! Those rooms were indeed restored later, but since there were sixty stone steps from the ground floor to the top room, with still more stone stairs leading to the water tank at the top of the tower, it became obvious that Ian would have spent more time and effort reaching his office than the time he might actually work there. Needless to say, he would abandon the idea, although the two bedrooms were rebuilt and are now enjoyed by guests and students.

The old courtyard was most typical of grand houses from the Victorian era with its horse stables on two sides—straw still remained in the mangers and hay in the lofts above. Under an impressive clock tower, we walked through a huge archway and a broken-down door leading to other parts of the property, including the large kitchen garden where flowers and vegetables had once been grown by hard-working gardeners for the resident family and their many visiting friends. Above the archway were some small rooms now fallen into disrepair, parts of which lay on the ground below. I found out later that this had been "home" for the head stableman and his family. On another side of the courtyard there was also, surprisingly, a type of garage large enough to have housed a few cars, but possibly the family's horse-drawn carriages had been kept in this area.

On meeting an elderly gentleman one day in the local town after we had lived at Capernwray for some weeks, I discovered that he had been a driver of what was probably an early Ford car that Colonel Marton's wife once owned. He related that when he had driven the lady to town in the morning, if she wished to use the car again in the afternoon of the same day for a visit to friends, Mrs. Marton insisted that it should always be cleaned and polished a second time before she would take her leave of Capernwray Hall.

On the third side of the courtyard was the servants' entrance to their own quarters. These and other buildings surrounded a huge area covered with cobblestones, and one could well imagine a busy morning for the stableman, with the clatter of horses' hooves, as the workers prepared the horses to take the "gentry" for a day's hunting on the large Capernwray estate.

By this time, we had explored other areas of the main house and were ready, finally, to retire for the night. Ian and I fully realized that an immense task lay ahead, the result of which we believed to be of God's design, and which He would accomplish as we were prepared to keep our trust firmly and obediently in Him. "Be strong and let your heart take courage, all you who hope IN the LORD." (Ps. 31:24, NASB, emphasis added)

Getting Started—But How?

Furniture and carpeting in every room, curtains for those high windows, kitchen and office equipment, not to mention the necessary staff, and much more would be required as soon as possible if we were to open those big, welcoming doors to our first guests the next summer, which was only six months away! What about funding for all of this? Where would we start once we had some money? Well, we certainly felt no panic but rather, believing that this place was God's and He would indeed provide, we thanked Him and slept gratefully and peacefully.

In his younger days as a traveling evangelist before the war, Ian had truly discovered God's provision for his every need. He told me once that on a particular occasion he had gone to a certain town in the north of England for an evangelistic mission in his tiny two-seater car. Arriving about a mile short of the outskirts of the town, he found the car needed gas, which we call "petrol" in the United Kingdom. He had no money for it, however, so he parked the car in a side street and walked the rest of the way to his destination. He told nobody, but he knew that God knew His need. Halfway through the first week of meetings, a lady, in thanking Ian for his ministry, handed him a "ten shilling note," (about seventy-five cents in US currency now) and Ian simply walked back the mile to that side street and put gas in his car. That was a good and useful experience. Until now, I believe that God, Ian and I were the only ones who knew that story.

Hudson Taylor, who founded the China Inland Mission—now OMF—wrote a daily devotional book which Ian stet in his early Christian life and which I discovered among some old papers. Hudson Taylor's experience as a pioneer missionary, who was confronted by challenges far bigger and more threatening than ours, nevertheless encouraged us when he quoted from 2 Chronicles 20:12: "Neither know we what to do: but our eyes are upon thee" (KJV).

Then Taylor wrote: "If God places me in great perplexity, must He not give me much guidance; in positions of great difficulty, much grace; in circumstances of great pressure and trial, much strength? No fear that His resources will be unequal to the emergency! And His resources are mine, for He is mine and is with me and dwells in me."[2]

Ian and I believed God would provide resources for opening Capernwray Hall as He had done for Hudson Taylor in China, so we were reminded that our eyes must always be on His greatness.

Important Beginnings

We were so grateful that Ian's eldest brother Geoffrey, an architect, kindly came from London on the second day that Ian could be at Capernwray before he was required to return to his responsibilities in Velbert, Germany. Geoffrey could give professional advice on some of the immediate and important structural alterations needing to be made in the big house.

In the meantime, with a small scrap of paper in hand, Ian took no time in numbering some of the usable bedrooms and in planning how many beds could be fitted, reasonably, into each room. These huge bedrooms were originally designed for one or two persons, but it is likely that the massive furniture of the time filled up the empty spaces. Now Ian was writing down:

"Dormitory number 1, 17 beds! number 4, maybe 15!" Then came a smaller room for seven beds, next, "Dorm 7, maybe 4 or 5!" There followed other "dormitories" of varying sizes, as well as a few small rooms for possibly two, which had been used by servants who had worked at Capernwray. Ian also had in mind the idea of converting the haylofts into bedrooms, as well as repairing the head stableman's quarters for accommodations in the courtyard. It became obvious that, with considerable faith, we were to prepare for at least one hundred or more young people to be our guests in the days ahead!

There was now no question that this magnificent mansion to which God had obviously led us for His purposes and for His glory would require huge changes, but its grand beauty should be unspoiled by modernization or the addition of further buildings. The local government had recorded Capernwray Hall as a "listed building" due to its historic interest so that alterations, in particular on the outside of the Hall, always required the permission of those officials.

The Marton family, previous owners of Capernwray, would probably have dated their origins to the Norman invasion of England from France in 1066. Colonel George Marton had Capernwray Hall built about the year 1840 on some of the land which he owned in Lancashire and where there was still part of an older building remaining. This aristocratic family lived in their grand house, cared for by a staff of some thirty servants, including, I was told, seven gardeners, cooks and kitchen maids, housemaids, a butler and many others. In every bedroom there was a bell, which was designed to send a message to the kitchen that a maid was required in that particular room. Yes, many changes needed to take place to convert this grand and imposing mansion to a place where crowds of young people, and older ones also, would feel at home and be given a warm and kindly welcome. Above all, it was our deepest desire that our guests—whoever they were and from whatever country they might come—would find the peace and joy of the presence of our living Lord Jesus, whose home it was, that they might come to know Him in new and life-changing ways.

During Ian's leave in November 1946, he and Geoffrey spent another day around the buildings. Then we visited the cottages on the property. In the "Gardener's Cottage" we met Mr. Dixon, his wife and family. Mr. Dixon had been Colonel Marton's estate manager and was now very willing to continue to maintain the extensive grounds and to help us generally in other ways. He remained as a valuable member of the staff for many years. One of the Dixons' two daughters was named Grace; and since she had recently left school, we were glad to have her help soon after our arrival in those first early days and later as permanent staff in the Capernwray office. For those who may read this book and who happen to have known Capernwray well, you may realize that this was Grace who married Billy Strachan.

In another of the cottages, I met Miss Hearne. She too was willing to continue her service even for the strange people who had now taken over the Hall. When this lady first came to work, it was obvious I was expected to address her as "Miss Hearne," and although we became good friends, she normally and very politely addressed me as "Madam." Small in stature, Miss Hearne's large white apron seemed to cover her whole body. Sometimes she wore a white cap. Scrubbing by hand two long flights of stone stairs on her knees was no problem for this small but strong lady. Miss Hearne had worked hard and thoroughly—she told me—under the eye of Mrs. Marton. I was surprised to find that even in 1946, living in a little cottage situated at one of Capernwray's main gates, Miss Hearne had still neither running water nor electricity in the house. She collected water from a nearby stream and cooked on a small open fire for herself and her brother who had been employed as one of the gardeners.

My diary for November 9 tells me that Ian spent time with the surveyor on that day, so some important beginnings had been going on as he and Geoffrey continued to draw up plans for work in and around the buildings.

I had also noted in the diary that we had a visit that very day from a young lady from Liverpool, about sixty miles from Capernwray. Joyce had requested an interview to become a secretary for us. Happily, she recently had come to know Christ as her Savior at an evangelistic crusade held in her city by none other than Ian's good friend, Tom Rees. Not having a true Christian home, Joyce felt Capernwray would be a place where she could learn more about her Lord, and enjoy fellowship with other believers. We were delighted to welcome her, especially as she went on to set up our office. Presently we had set aside one end of our living room in the old "smoking room" with a typewriter and some packets of writing paper. Later, the original butler's pantry located near the front of the house was to become the main office. It lacked heating, however, and Joyce's fingers often "froze" on her typewriter. By working around the house and burning pieces of wood in the fireplaces, we managed to keep somewhat warm in what was then reported to be in England "the coldest winter in living memory."

Geoffrey had to leave for London and Ian to return for his final five weeks in the Army of Occupation in Germany, leaving me, my mother, and sister Mary, in sole charge of the Hall. Our small son delighted in running around his dad's "big house," exploring and finding what he called "new" rooms.

It was an interesting and ongoing experience working long days, scrubbing and painting here, there and everywhere. Because Mary and I did not have a car, or any way to go to town for shopping, we rode our bicycles to the nearby railway station for the one train of the day which stopped there to run errands. We always felt important when the stationmaster welcomed us with a tip of his cap, now that we lived like those aristocratic Martons at Capernwray Hall. Then he would assist us by his friendly hand into the railway carriage. Those were the days!

Despite all the fears I had of "living in a big house with lots of young people," God somehow gave the joy of looking forward to what He had in His heart for the days, possibly years, ahead and I believed it must be good. Had He not already told me in Psalm 31:19 that His goodness was already "stored up"—as good as done—if I would but trust Him and, in verse 24, to be of good courage, and He would give strength for the task? That He did.

The very last entry in my diary for 1946, the last one I ever again had the time to keep, was on Thursday, December 5. I wrote it in large letters, surrounded by many extra lines: "IAN'S DE-MOB [demobilization]. CHRISTOPHER'S BIRTHDAY."

What a day that was for us to offer the deepest gratitude to almighty God for a safe return from a terrible world war, when many thousands of others had died in battle, leaving their loved ones to sorrow at home.

For us, it was also a day to thank God for the small son He had given us, for whom we would often pray that in growing up at Capernwray Hall, he would learn to love Jesus and to serve Him with all his heart. The coming years were to see these prayers fully answered as God in His goodness allowed Chris and later Mark to experience Bible school training in the United

States. Many years later, Stuart Briscoe, who in God's good time was to be such a part of Capernwray, invited Chris to be associate pastor with him at Elmbrook Church, Milwaukee where for four years, our son gained valuable experience. It came as no surprise when Ian assigned Chris to become general director for all worldwide Capernwray ministries. This important ministry continues to be his, involving constant travel, teaching, and personal involvement with staff and associates, which Chris manages with much ability and enthusiasm.

Goodness Stored Up

That great day, we celebrated Ian's demobilization and Christopher's birthday as best we could since food rationing meant we had inadequate ingredients for a homemade birthday cake. However, to make a "sponge cake" in wartime, we had become used simply to mixing dried egg and dried milk with flour, none of which were rationed, with a little water and a sprinkle of sugar. The oven did the rest. Then, though we had neither seen nor eaten a banana since before the war, I had been given the recipe for banana sandwiches for the birthday party by boiling parsnips until soft, then mixing them with a fork and adding some banana essence. We spread the results between slices of bread, and we all ate them just as they were.

Ian had little time for celebrating the end of army service with all the work that lay ahead. He was soon to be seen walking excitedly around the big, mostly empty house and planning, as God directed him, how to change its purpose and its title to "Capernwray Christian Holiday Conference Center."

We were to celebrate Ian's war service in style some weeks later as Ian's mother and I, the only two guests allowed, were driven in a large black London taxi through the open gates of

Buckingham Palace to the fine main entrance. There we were led to our seats in the grand Reception Hall to witness King George V himself pin a DSO—Distinguished Service Order—medal on Ian's army jacket. Part of the citation for this award read that Major Thomas "was everywhere to be found encouraging his men and by his presence and his indifference to heavy small arms fire . . . inspiring them," and that "he handled the battalion with the greatest skill and daring."

The challenges of a very different kind and in a very different world now lay ahead.

Obviously, the initial challenge was simply that of finance. Another was the discovery that as a result of World War II, the British Government was limiting, to the point of severity, the amount of money that could be spent on private homes. Priority had to be given to the reconstruction of schools, hospitals, government offices and other essential buildings. This restriction was due to the heavy loss, or damage, to many such buildings in war-time air raids, as well as to the lack of materials. We would have to apply for a license, and we hardly qualified at Capernwray Hall.

Somehow, a fine Christian bank manager heard of our need and offered to give some helpful advice. He had a friend whose interest was in a large hotel whose owner was about to purchase a new stove for its kitchen. We could have the old stove, which was still usable. Since there was no stove for cooking in the large Capernwray kitchen, this was indeed a helpful gift. These two gentlemen came by car to visit the Hall, and upon their arrival at one of the main gates, they couldn't continue since their car became firmly stuck in the snow. This was but the beginning of a very snowy winter in England, and it was a challenge living in our large unheated mansion. Those two kind gentlemen trudged by foot up the long drive to the Hall where we welcomed them as warmly as we could. God was showing us already His promised "goodness" in a very practical and much needed way. A short time later, Gordon, who had joined with Ian and others in Velbert, Germany, for prayer and Bible study, came to join us on staff. Having been preparing pre-war to become a certified public accountant, Gordon's professional help was most welcome at this time.

During the time when Ian was still involved in war service in Germany, not knowing the events which would actually take place so soon after his return home, he had accepted invitations to speak at evangelistic meetings early in 1947. These he could not now cancel. Those of us on "the staff" were left at Capernwray to work our long days, and for Mary and me, sometimes into the night with our painting and scrubbing. We often teased Ian about escaping hard work.

Northern Ireland, where Ian would be preaching, was familiar territory for him. He had many friends there who had prayed for him during the war years and who were now anxious to know his future plans. On hearing about the possibilities for using Capernwray Hall as a base for sharing the gospel in the context of a good holiday, the people became excited, offering to help in many ways. Some of them invested their savings in the work while others donated furniture, chairs, curtains and many other important household items. Army beds were made available with their horsehair mattresses—not the most comfortable for a good night's sleep, but very gratefully received. In the coming days, God seemed to bring much of what we needed out of His storehouse through many of our good friends. At various other places where Ian had the opportunity to preach, the story was the same.

God also added His blessing to the preaching of His life-changing Word so that souls were saved and, following the horrors of a world war, it was obviously now a perfect time to proclaim that the answer to peace with God was in the Life-giver alone, the Lord Jesus. We believed that Capernwray could become a place of blessing to our guests where many would come to acknowledge Him as Lord and Savior. God did indeed "do it" over many years, through hundreds of His people who would offer their hands and their hearts for the work.

In the mail one day, we received a custard tin wrapped up in brown paper that contained, not custard powder, but two hundred UK pound notes. The kind donor still remains anonymous. Ian's parents, opposed at one time to their son having left medical studies to become a common traveling "preacher," now delighted in the work we were developing at Capernwray Hall, especially as it would benefit young people. His parents became most generous in their financial support.

Soon the time came when we needed to apply for a building license in order to install bathrooms, make changes in the large kitchen, and prepare offices, in addition to many other projects .In the north of England and based in the city of Manchester, the head of the Ministry of Works responsible for granting licenses was an ex-army officer named Brigadier Temple. Ian, as an ex-army major, used his "military might" to encourage this gentleman to come to Capernwray to see for himself what exactly our essential and immediate building requirements were. Meanwhile, Ian's father and brother Geoffrey, both architects, had kindly traveled overnight by train from London to Carnforth to assess the amount of funding it would require to make the necessary internal changes in the main building in order to accommodate, we hoped, at least one hundred young people.

After his "grand tour" of the buildings, the brigadier granted that we could use half of the amount requested. We considered this a good outcome and gave thanks not only to him, but above all, to the Lord Himself. Had the answer been that Capernwray did not qualify, we would have had a big problem to face, but it became clear that God was on our side, as we were on His.

Provision and Progress

The first three months of 1947 were truly exciting as we saw Capernwray Hall gradually move toward the purpose for which we had "gone a little further" at the auction in the Lancaster Town Hall on September 11, 1946. To swing open those big oak doors at the front of the building and welcome our first young people was a moment we eagerly anticipated. Nevertheless, there was so very much still to be done, and we needed more workers to help us do it.

We were wonderfully provided with a vehicle, what we then referred to as a "shooting brake" but is known in the United States as a pickup truck. This was a Ford V-8, old, large and powerful enough for our needs. God also provided a hard-working young man to maintain and drive it, who was also willing to do much else beside. Geoffrey Gilboy had seen army service during the war years, and he arrived at just the right time. He quickly set to work covering the ugly khaki color on the iron army bed frames with two coats of light cream paint. It was quite a sight to see the cobblestoned courtyard covered with beds. We hoped none of our guests would arrive early and think they were to sleep outdoors!

Plumbers also came to add some much-needed bathrooms, followed by carpenters, who fitted cupboards for bedrooms out of the wood of library shelves that we no longer required in the big lounge that the Martons had used as a library. It was good to find that one large bedroom and the billiard room both had fitted carpets still remaining, and we purchased some for other rooms. We were making progress.

Soon, many friends heard that Capernwray Hall, near the beautiful English Lake District, was to be opened as a residential Christian youth center, and we received offers of help from people willing to work on staff. Ian had contacted a business friend in the south of England, with whom he had shared ministry before the war, a man who was willing to assist in administration. His name was Leonard Van Dooren, with family origins in Belgium. Our children named him "Uncle Van" and he remained, working faithfully at Capernwray, for many years, and he was an essential part of the whole fellowship until his retirement.

Arriving in good time to prepare the big kitchen and become our first cook was Irma, along with Cherrie from Ireland, and Jean, who took care of the big house. Brenda, who had attended Bible studies and prayer times in Velbert, Germany, and who was a well-trained nurse, also joined staff as our manageress. Other young people came, ready and willing to do anything to support the exciting new ministry. Yes, God provided just as He had promised He would.

The big dining room, with its fine black marble fireplace and high windows, became the important meeting room, and we employed some green canvas-seated chairs to accommodate our guests. We had enough for one hundred, although it took some months to reach that number. As a dining area we prepared the old billiard room, finding tables and chairs available from a war-time army tea room. The kitchen, also in the process of being prepared, was some distance along a stone corridor, but not nearly as far as the servants for the Marton family, who'd had to carry many dishes with huge silver covers to the dining room at the front of the building.

By this time, Joyce was preparing the main office, where the head butler had once ruled the household, and from where he had welcomed local gentry, who would have arrived at the front of the house in carriages drawn by their well-groomed horses. We were surprised and glad to find that a telephone was already installed in the butler's pantry, probably for the benefit of the headmaster of the school that had occupied Capernwray during the war years. Our good friend Gordon was also working in the office while Ian was preparing the very first brochure for the "Capernwray Christian Holiday Conference Center." We planned to open on Saturday, May 10, with the first conference, and then to arrange subsequent weekly ones until October. Ian had many wonderful Christian friends around the country, whom he knew would present a true Christ-centered message, making the gospel clear from God's Word, so he had no trouble finding a speaker for each week. There were many already in Christian ministry from various denominations, including missionaries, a doctor, a school teacher and others who were happy to be a part of this new ministry. We purchased copies of the then-popular "Golden Bells" hymnal, and my mother was ready and very happy, as a well-trained piano teacher and a good accompanist, to play her part at every meeting. Apart from much else besides, our heavenly Father had provided members of staff who were willing to be a vital part of the project and to work hard with little reward.

So it was that by early April, looking back on the previous hectic months, that we could see how our gracious God had made provision for Ian's deep desire and my initial dread—to find a "big house where we could have lots of young people to stay." By His enabling and His Presence in that house, they were able to find the reality of the Christian life, not a religion nor a doctrine, but a Person—Christ Himself.

The office telephone proved to be most useful as soon as we had arrived at Capernwray Hall back in November 1946. At that time, living, as it seemed, in the back of beyond, not having transport and unable to know how or where to obtain various materials and many other things, it was a blessing to find a voice at the other end of the old telephone. One had first to pick up the telephone, turn a small handle a few times on the side of the stand, then the operator would answer immediately with a cheery "hello." He could always answer my inquiries. One day I asked the operator—it was always the same one with the friendly voice—if he could give me the name and phone number of a local doctor because I was living at Capernwray Hall and would be having a baby before long. So it was that early in April, about a month before Geoffrey was to drive our first guests to Capernwray, the doctor arrived, and a little son was born in room number twenty—a brother for Chris. Both little brother Mark and I were ready to welcome the very first guests. Our sons spent their early years growing up at Capernwray and attending the local village school. Many years later and after high school, both Mark and Chris attended Bible college in the United States. For some time, Mark ministered as a youth pastor there. Then, many years later, when Ian and I were soon to move away, the day came when Ian nominated Mark as the director of Capernwray Hall. So it is that Mark continues to welcome many guests, now from around the world, besides having himself a ministry in Europe and elsewhere.

Provision—yes. Progress—yes. To God be the glory—soon those big front doors would be thrown open to receive our very first guests.

4

The Start of Torchbearing

The weekly summer conferences that we started in May were to begin and end on Saturdays, continuing throughout the summer until October. We placed small advertisements in Christian magazines, and Joyce in the office received an initial ten applications. So it was that in my mother's diary I find the simple words, "Capernwray opened—10 guests." We had at that time about thirteen willing workers, thus outnumbering our guests.

On Saturday, May 10, 1947, Geoffrey was ready with the "brake" to bring the very first visitor from the railway station, a woman named Mary. On entering through the big front doors, Joyce came out to meet and welcome her while Geoffrey looked for me somewhere in the building to ask which room he should take her to. I believe I told him room five. Having taken Mary, with her small suitcase, up the long stairway to her quarters, Geoffrey then asked what he should do for her next. I suggested that as it would be some time before he would be meeting the rest of our guests, he might, if she wished to do so, walk with Mary around the rose garden, where there was a lily pond and even a few early roses. I believe he did so—and, as I often tell our young people, Geoffrey and Mary have been walking together ever since—they married just a few years later! Theirs has been the experience of very many other married couples who have had the joy of meeting each other in the atmosphere of Christian surroundings like Capernwray.

The rest of our guests duly arrived, were welcomed to our big house, and taken to their dormitories where, we hoped, they would get a sound night's sleep on those iron beds. We always had a good cup of tea awaiting them in the main lounge, followed by an evening meal. Although it was fully two years after the war, England was still experiencing food rationing; I believe we were the last of the allied countries to be "unrationed." Our guests were required to bring their ration books with them so that, having accounted for the meals and beverages served each week, we then took a report to the local food office and our ration for the following week would be assessed. This was quite complicated! For the cooks, it was never easy to provide delicious meals with the small weekly allowance of some essential foods.

Early in the summer, a retired friend, who had been in the grocery business, came to help at Capernwray. Besides his excellent ministry to our young people, counseling and leading some to Christ, Mr. Taylor was an expert at growing mushrooms. He found the old and quite extensive damp and dark cellars at Capernwray, which our children called dungeons, perfect for his hobby, and our guests benefited. They could have mushrooms on toast for breakfast, mushroom soup at lunch, and maybe more mushrooms included in the evening meal. No rationing— and no complaints in those old days.

It was such a joy to experience the first ever meeting at "Capernwray Hall Christian Holiday Conference Center." Welcoming our first guests—even a few—and being introduced to each other, with much hearty singing, was but the beginning of God's plan for the coming years at the big house. Ian led the first meetings, and in his absence, "Uncle Van" did so. He became a friend to many and always delighted in opportunities to lead young folk to Christ and to be available for conversation.

Mother noted in her diary on Wednesday of the second week: "One guest (Liverpool girl) saved this p.m." Then on Friday: "3 (Liverpool) guests accepted Christ's salvation tonight." "And good for Liverpool too," I thought! Then the first week of June she noted, "Fine week, several saved, including Albert (aged 19)." So the weeks continued with fine teaching from our speakers and the joy of fellowship together.

The only sports that we had available in those early days were tennis on an old, often wet, grass court, or a game of croquet on the big lawn at the back of the main house. Table tennis was also popular for those who were willing and able to climb up to one of the haylofts where they would find the table, paddles and balls. The Lake District was a great place to visit, and around Capernwray there were pleasant walks and very few cars on the narrow roads at that time. Within a couple of years, we purchased three horses so that our guests could experience the pleasure of horse riding. Most had never ridden before, so Brenda and I, with our well-stocked medicine cupboard, were sometimes called upon to make use of our nursing experience. At least those old cobblestones in the courtyard echoed once more to the clatter of horses' hoofs.

The Increase

It was most encouraging to find that each week there was an increase in the number of guests coming to experience a Christian holiday at Capernwray. From the first week of ten, the number increased to twenty-one, then to fifty-four, seventy, and by the 20th of July, 1947, as my mother recorded in her diary: "Guest speaker Geoffrey King (London) great blessing—over 90 guests." We were blessed to have speakers whose names are still familiar through their writings, including Arthur Wallis and Roy Hession. Friday nights were always what we called "Say So" nights, named from Psalm 107:2, "Let the redeemed of the Lord say so." It was a joy to hear many genuine testimonies from those who already knew Christ as Savior, some of whom had entered into a new and deeper relationship with Him during the week of meetings. There were also guests who had come to Capernwray without knowing Christ, but on understanding the simple truth of the gospel message, had clearly and joyfully received Him by simple faith. We were very amused to hear a young boy at one of the "say so" meetings testify that he had come to Christ "on the back of a horse."

As I mentioned earlier, one of the activities for our guests at Capernwray soon after we had opened the Center was horse riding. The rides were normally led, if not by a young man who had been invited to join staff especially to be in charge of the horses and lead the riding, then by others—maybe Gordon or Ian might do so. In the case of this young boy, Ian was riding alongside, explaining as they rode, how he could come to know the Lord Jesus for himself—and that boy was born again.

Over the years since Capernwray Hall first opened, we have heard from, and met very many friends, missionaries, pastors, Bible teachers and others who were led to Christ at what Ian once described as "a large house somewhere so that we can have lots of young people to stay and teach them the truth about the Christian life."

Cassells Morrell, who came to Capernwray from Northern Ireland at the age of thirteen, was just such a young person. Traveling with a large group of teenagers from his home church, it was the first time he had been out of his country and away from, his home on a small farm. Finding his way to the "Beehive" snack bar in the old Capernwray courtyard, Cassells recalled later: "Major stopped me and asked if I was a Christian. Twenty minutes later and after some discussion and prayer in Major's study (formerly Colonel Marton's smoking room) and by God's mercy and grace, I had passed from death to Life." Just a boy of thirteen, that boy studied, worked hard and continues part time as the associate secretary for Europe with the Fellowship of International Students. Cassells preaches often and also has a key position in his local church as a team leader doing pastoral care. As Ian used to say, "If you wait long enough, boys will become men and girls will become women and the kind they become depends on the kind they were." Even in our current fallen world, God continues to seek out even the young and insignificant. May Torchbearers find them.

God graciously continued to meet our needs through the support of many of our visiting friends. On one occasion, a farmer was among those who had booked to stay for a week. He was so blessed as the result of his visit that he made an arrangement to give the proceeds from one of his fields to support the work at Capernwray. This particular field was normally planted with turnips, so it became the "Capernwray turnip field," and it yielded a rich harvest for us.

We praise God that He has used the ministry at Capernwray through many of His servants, who have helped to support financially. There are many other stories like the "turnip field" one. He has also provided over the years very many of those who have given much hard physical labor in all departments of the Center. Through these and more, God has indeed provided a harvest for His glory.

The Germans Are Coming!

Having received our first guests, numbering just ten, in May of 1947, we trusted our Lord God to add to that number during the following weeks of the summer, and we were not disappointed. He had provided for Capernwray until that point, and we believed He would continue to do so. We were overjoyed to see His hand of blessing in the lives of those who came to know Christ for themselves, even as others were encouraged to know Him better during their stay at the Hall. Mary, the first ever guest to arrive at the "new" Capernwray Hall, and who later married Geoffrey the "brake" driver, has returned with him and the family since then. We continue to keep in touch with others from the early years, though now they are quite old. One of the guests from that first group was called to missionary service in Africa during her stay that very first week.

God not only provides, but sometimes He surprises us by the way He provides. Once the summer conferences ended that October, only the staff remained, working on the building and in the grounds. Some were able to spend Christmas at their homes, but it seemed to be "bad for business" with no guests and no income in sight for the ongoing expenses at the Hall. However, early in 1948, God had His surprise ready to be revealed in the form of a letter to Ian from the British Foreign Office in London. It explained how the government desired to find a way to rebuild relationships and promote reconciliation between the youth of Germany and those in England following the years of horror and hatred between our two nations. Those government officials in London had an idea—that British Welfare and Education Officers were to specially select German young people to come to England, at government expense, to spend a month in a suitable place where they would meet and share time together with British youth. Officials in London had approached a friend of ours, who directed a camping program for boys during the summer months. He was unable to help, however, and suggested that they might contact "Major Thomas at Capernwray Hall, a big house in the north west of England." This was surely a God-given opportunity to show in a very practical way the conviction Ian had described in one of the letters he'd written to me from Velbert: "God loves Germans, Jesus died for Germans and we are going to love them too."

Arrangements were soon made for us to host German young people at Capernwray Hall for a visit of one month during the summer of 1948. I well remember entering that big lounge where, in previous days, only a handful of the Marton family and their friends reclined in their comfortable couches and arm-chairs. Now the room hosted a group of German young folks, along with a few British guests, around the fireplace. Some even sat on the floor—the Germans not quite knowing what we were about to do to them! At the same time, I was thinking how strange it seemed that though our armies had been fighting each other only months ago, now we were to love and understand these guests, feed and come to know them and, most of all, lead them to know Jesus Christ personally. Then we could send them home to be a means of blessing in their own country, especially to their families and friends.

Naturally, our English guests first found it somewhat unexpected to share their mealtimes, the twice daily meetings in the conference hall, and their occasional excursions and walks with these "strangers" and former enemies. However, the British officials had selected young Germans who had a fair knowledge of spoken English, and as far as could be understood, those who'd had a good education and who showed possible leadership qualities. Ian requested the authorities that Eberhard Witte, whose home was the first Ian had requisitioned when he was stationed in Velbert, should be invited to be part of the group of thirty, along with two of his friends. This resulted in a further strengthening of Ian's many contacts with Christians in that German town. Having Eberhard as a guest in *our* home was perhaps a small recompense for Ian having sent the family away from theirs to live in the factory, so some army officers could enjoy comfortable quarters. Eberhard came to Christ during his stay at Capernwray and many years later was, for a short time before his death, a member of the board at one of the Torchbearer Centres in Germany.

The British authorities paid Capernwray for the stay of the German young people, requiring only that they should have the opportunity to mix freely with our English guests and that they should be given occasional lectures in the law and practice of democratic government. The Germans were expected to attend meetings morning and evening and to accept our normal house rules. The British learned to sing a few choruses in German, and vice versa. Within days, friendships with various other British guests and the staff blossomed. These German young folk had suffered, as we had, the loss of family members, friends and homes during the war years. They were disillusioned, disappointed and distressed about the past seven years, and frightened about the future. A few were already believers and church members, but all were open to receive the kindness and understanding given to them in the name of the Lord Jesus, and through hearing His Word. The first German guest to receive Christ as her Savior had sat in the back row at one of the meetings in tears. One of our secretaries, who sat beside her, had the joy of leading Amie to Christ as they walked the grounds afterwards. During their stay at Capernwray many others in the German group, having heard the good news of the gospel spelled out clearly in the power of the Holy Spirit, responded and received Christ with open hearts. One was Ilse, whom "Uncle"—Mr. Taylor, the mushroom grower—led to Christ.

Following Ilse's return to Germany, her brother Horst, a theological student, made his own arrangements with the British "Education Branch," which was still active in Germany, to visit Capernwray Hall in 1949. We kept Horst's original report of that visit, dated February 2, 1949, which he mailed to the authorities, and was then forwarded by them to Major Thomas. Reading Horst's words, carefully translated into English, we can now realize that the plans the British authorities had made in order to "find a way to rebuild relationships and to promote reconciliation between British and German youth" had, in fact, their origins in the heart of God long before we bid that "little bit further" at the auction. Surely, as the psalmist wrote, "As for God, HIS way is perfect" (Ps. 18:30, KJV, emphasis added).

Here is an excerpt from two long pages of Horst's account. He began: "I do not claim that this report on my trip to England is in any way complete, being fully conscious that the report can in no wise do justice to what has been experienced by me. This brotherhood is difficult to depict—it has to have been experienced. And if I attempt none the less to depict it and the blessings it has brought to many, I must crave indulgence for the incompleteness of the picture."

He continued: "First of all the word brotherhood needs explanation and how it all came about. How is it possible that two men who were fighting against one another so bitterly five or six years ago can now not only sit down together peaceably—that you may say has happened in other cases as well—but more than that, become brothers and dwelt together and cherished one another as such. This was brought about through the propagation of the Word of God. All who heard and accepted the Word by opening their hearts to receive it became one great family.

"You were not asked 'Whence comest thou?' What mattered was 'Whither goest thou?' And this question was meant to ascertain if the objective was the Kingdom of God. Then whether we were English, Swiss or Germans was completely beside the point. No communism held sway, yet all there was there was shared in common in a wonderful spirit of harmony. Brotherly love dictated that I did not play tennis just because I wanted to—and it was the same with the others. The same harmony persisted in all everyday affairs. No 'I want to' dictated our actions; they were governed by the love for one's neighbor. I knew my Redeemer Jesus Christ before my trip to England, but had no idea that life in a community which recognized Him as their Master could be such a real thing. I think of the celebration of the Lord's Supper. How well I know as a theological student of the various interpretations that have led to quarrels among the theologians of the different confessions. Yet here were sitting together not only brothers in faith of different confessions such as the Church of England, Baptists, Methodists and others, but a mixture of nations such as I have never experienced before. English, Dutch, French, Americans, Swiss, Germans—all were represented. Each thought in his mother tongue yet were all one in Him our Lord. There was no need for a conference as to whether this or that was possible or not—we saw that it was possible and also experienced the fact that it was so.

"Each morning and evening this community sought fresh adjustment and guidance through a preacher who expounded the Word of the Bible. By this means such as were conscious that they were not yet fully united with all the others as brothers in the Lord could be shown the road leading to HIM."

When our friend Horst Fuhrmeister became a pastor in Germany, he then brought German young people to Capernwray on many occasions to share in the summer conferences so that they too might find their own way to a living relationship with Jesus Christ.

Friedrich Thöele had a desire after the war to become a politician in Germany, so the British authorities invited him to study democratic institutions in Great Britain. After a time in the town of Leeds to study town council work, Friedrich was told to proceed to Capernwray Hall to study the "functioning of a youth center." He wrote afterward, "There I was welcomed by Major Thomas, his wife Joan and the Secretary Vera Porter." Vera happened to be the same secretary who led that tearful girl Amie to Christ. Friedrich said of his experience at Capernwray: "I often talked with Vera about religious topics and eventually on the 15th of June 1948 we read in the *Daily Light*, 'The Spirit . . . maketh intercession for the saints according to the will of God. Verily, verily I say unto you . . .' Vera and I kneeled and she asked me the decisive question: 'Friedrich, won't you accept the Lord Jesus as your personal Savior and you will be born again?' I said YES! And I have never regretted it to this day."

It didn't take long before our German young folk began to feel at home, to appreciate the kindness they received and the friendliness and interest of the other guests. Some of our local Christian friends began to attend the evening meetings, and together we sang our hymns and choruses. When needed, the evening message was translated into German in a side room with the door ajar, there being few electronic devices or headphones sixty years ago. One day a very kind Christian friend from a nearby village, who owned a small shoe shop, arrived with the trunk of his car filled with boots and shoes in order to fit each one of our young German guests with footwear. Needless to say, there was great rejoicing among them, since they possessed only the one pair of shoes they were wearing.

These were busy and tiring, but thrilling days as we had occasion to look back and trace God's hand on our lives from our earliest years. As a boy of twelve, Ian had come to a moment of decision to receive Christ, then at nineteen he allowed God to direct his life in totality. Then, through six years of preaching the gospel in his own country and seven years of war, the same God had now fulfilled his deepest longing. Ian finally had a big house filled with young people where they would have the opportunity to give themselves wholly to Jesus Christ and receive back His indwelling life, a life that will never die.

This passion had always filled Ian's heart. Many years earlier he wrote: "May His love fill us more and more with Calvary zeal in winning lost souls to Him. Life has no value except in terms of souls saved, and Christians quickened to a fuller realization and enjoyment of the spiritual 'completeness' which is to be found in Him, in whom dwelleth all the fullness of the Godhead bodily."

No wonder, then, that Ian found himself happily involved in talking and praying personally, often after the meetings and late into the night, with many of the guests who stayed in Capern-wray. Numbers of the British and the Germans came to Christ, and others were encouraged and blessed. After four weeks of solid teaching from the Word of God, many of the German young people began to be really excited about returning home to share the joy of knowing Christ in a personal way with others, a joy they had never known before. In fact, it was they who first applied the word "Torchbearers" to their group, or in German, "Fackelträger," meaning "Carriers of the Light." In other words they carried the light of Christ within them back home to friends, family and, for some, to school. After twelve years of Nazi dictatorship, indoctrination, abuse, and finally the collapse and defeat of the system, the German young people were disillusioned, as well as morally and spiritually neglected. Being shown Christ's love in the person of a former enemy must have been overwhelming for many adolescents who witnessed the horrors of the final months of the war, especially those who had been forcibly recruited to defend the country, sometimes as young as thirteen or fourteen. I am sure that God used these events to open doors to the gospel.

What can we say but that "God did it?" All praise to Him!

Returning to Germany

Following the busy summer of 1948, our second at Capern-wray Hall, the staff remained busy. There was much cleaning to be done and many improvements to be made both inside and on the outside of our big house. God provided willing hands, including a man named Ted, a skilled builder whose first accomplishment was to renovate the two bedrooms in the main tower with its eighty steps from the ground floor. These were the rooms destroyed by fire years before, during the Marton's residency. Sometimes friends sent us various gifts, like curtains, furniture and even pictures for the bare walls, while others donated funds. We received everything most gratefully. Gordon and Ian began to plan a Christmas conference in addition to our summer schedule, and we also established a board of directors. Ian had already set up Capernwray Hall as a limited company.

In November of 1948, about one month before Christmas, another special and very welcome gift arrived when our local doctor delivered our third son in room twenty-one. We were so happy to add Peter to our little family. Peter grew up to study at a Torchbearer Bible School and went on to become a school master in the north of Wales before God sent him to the other side of the world to lead and direct the Torchbearer ministry in Australia and New Zealand. Peter continues as the director at "Monavale," the Torchbearer Centre south of Auckland, and he oversees the other Torchbearer Centres in the South Pacific area. Peter, with his Australian wife and their family, are a long way from our home, but he delights in following up on his dad's earlier ministry in New Zealand, and through him, God has continued to bless and extend Torchbearing throughout the country.

Our Christmas 1948 brochure attracted a number of guests for the conference, which was well attended and which the people thoroughly enjoyed. There was plenty of holly and greenery from the grounds for decorating the house, and the staff managed to string Christmas paper streamers across the high walls and up the big main staircase. We held morning and evening meetings, sang carols and played what would now be "old-fashioned" games. Father Christmas—Santa Claus—even appeared one evening, just as he has done at Capernwray ever since.

That December in England was very cold and even with log

fires burning in the huge fireplaces in the lounges, the house was frosty too, as were our guests. In the dark, damp cellar a large boiler, fueled with coke (a type of coal), had been installed years earlier, but it needed to be fired frequently. Ian set our alarm clock to waken him during the night so he could find his way in the darkness of the cellar, there being no lighting there at that time, and he would stoke the boiler with huge logs of wood, of which we had a good supply from the grounds. At least our guests could awaken in their rooms to a little warmth. Until we installed a very efficient oil boiler, hot water bottles were the order of the day—or night—and on cold nights, there were always a number of mostly women waiting in line to fill them from the large water boiler near the kitchen.

Following that very first Christmas at Capernwray, Ian decided that we should travel to Germany and visit, in their homes, as many as possible of the members of that first group of German young people who had stayed at Capernwray during the past summer. We had come to know and love them, and it was important to meet their families and friends and, above all else, Ian wanted to encourage them in their newfound relationship with Jesus Christ. So it was that with a list of names and addresses, having notified the young people that they should try to arrange gatherings of their friends and families, we set off by car early on February 10, 1949, to drive to Velbert, where Ian had spent over a year in the Army of Occupation, where we knew we would be welcomed at our "home away from home" with the Witte family.

Travel throughout the continent of Europe from England in 1949 was not as easy as it would become some years later. First, we had a long car journey from the north of England to Dover in the south without the benefit of dual motorways. Then there was a four-hour ferry crossing from Dover to Calais, France, followed by a long drive by car through Belgium and Holland, before we finally arrived in Velbert, Germany at our home with the Witte family at 84 Hindenburgstrasse.

When World War II first began, the German government had directed that at the main entrance to every town and city in the country, the name of that place was to be removed so that an enemy would be confused as to his whereabouts. These names had not yet been replaced, so it was not at all easy to find our way. We depended on enquiries to any passersby as to the location we sought. Fortunately, Ian had a fair knowledge of the German language so that he understood the directions we received. I did not know even one word, having studied only French at school. The first expression I quickly learned was "*immer gerade aus*," meaning "just straight on"—and that we did, for many miles.

Three years after the war was over, not only were certain foods still rationed in England, but due to the shortage of vehicles, it was not possible to purchase a car unless one had "priority." That meant you needed to be someone whose work was absolutely essential to the community, such as a doctor, nurse, member of the police or a government official. As a traveling evangelist and director of a large youth center, Ian found that having a vehicle was totally essential, if not crucial. He went to a car dealer, who told Ian that unless he possessed coupons for petrol, he could not purchase a car. Therefore, Ian went to an office that supplied the coupons only to be informed they could not be issued unless he had a car. Ian said he wondered why he had gone to war.

Some time later he tried again. On visiting a car dealer in Nottingham, where we had lived for a time, the dealer inquired what Ian's "priority" might be. Ian pointed to a picture hanging on the wall behind the dealer's desk depicting a huge ugly hand rising out of a stormy sea where each of the fingers was fighting with or strangling the one alongside; one with a spear was attempting to stab its neighbor. Under this ugly picture, which the car dealer, Mr. Ernest Shouls himself had cut out of a magazine, he had written the word "Mankind." Pointing to the picture Ian simply said, "That's my priority—God never made a hand like that." There followed a vital conversation with the salesman, which resulted a few days later in Mr. Shouls attending a meeting at which Ian was speaking in the home of a friend. The car dealer waited until everyone had left, and then he told Ian he needed God, and before long, he knelt at a chair in the room and gave his life to Christ. I still treasure a letter Ernest Shouls wrote to Ian many years later when the car dealer was a much older man living in a retirement home, reminding Ian of the day he found the answer, not only to his own need but to that of all mankind, a saving relationship with Jesus Christ. He closed the letter with the words, "I am still living in the power of God's Spirit."

Of course, and fortunately for us, the car we got was a Vauxhall, made in England. So it was that in that Vauxhall car we made the journey to Germany, arriving very late on Thursday, February 10, 1949, in Velbert. We were to stay about three weeks.

During our visits to some of the homes of the Capernwray group whom we had come to love and to know so well, we were very warmly received by their parents and treated like royalty. Their sufferings from the years of wartime were very obvious, yet they were extremely kind and shared their homes and the little that they had with us, their former enemies. Members of that first group who had stayed with us in 1948 arranged meetings in churches, schools and homes. The Witte home became our headquarters, as well as our home away from home. The following is a small but significant part of the original three-week itinerary and report of just a few of the meetings we held in various German towns.

Thursday, February 10th *Arriving Velbert*

Friday, February 11th *We traveled to Düsseldorf where Inge, who had been to Capernwray, had arranged a meeting and Ian writes in the report, "the discussion following the address showed that everybody was very interested."*

Back to Velbert through thick fog, arriving 11:30 p.m.

Sunday, February 13th *Meeting of about 600 to 800 boys and girls and the Free Churches. On the way home to Velbert, the foundation for Die Fackeltraeger was laid.*

Tuesday, February 15th *Meeting of a youth group in the Witte's home: Many questions asked and answered and many realized what they had been called to do.*

With no public announcement or boardroom meeting, but probably just by a simple discussion in the car, "Torchbearers" was born—a name which has now spread around the world. At later meetings in various towns and homes from which the Germans at Capernwray had come, Ian recorded attendances of, "about 70 in Dieter's home then about 200 to 300 people in a school and 170 boys and girls in a meeting of the Christian Youth groups in Dortmund."

More busy and exciting days followed. One in particular began in a boys' school at 8:00 in the morning and lasted until 5:00 in the evening, after which time there was a meeting of one hundred youngsters of the Christian Endeavour, followed, as Ian reported, by a "Big Rally with all the youth groups of Hattingen. Pastor Reimers, very good. Grand meeting, 30-40 accept Christ!" Then there were many discussions in peoples' homes, one of which ended at midnight and another about 2:00 a.m. At one place Ian wrote, "Many Roman Catholic boys looked into a Bible for the first time in their life."

Some of the members of our German youths must have, on returning home after being at Capernwray, shared the light and life of Christ with others. They were indeed "Fackeltraeger"— Torchbearers.

Nearing the end of this first post-war visit to Germany, it seemed that God was opening doors to establish a growing ministry among German youth and that this was but the small beginning of much more that He had in His heart. The entry in Ian's report, prior to our departure two days later, said it all.

> **Tuesday, March 7th** *Leaving Paderborn at 7 a.m. for Velbert. Arrive Velbert in the afternoon. Meeting of the first Fackeltraeger.*

Upon reflection, the name of "Torchbearers," or "Fackeltraeger," had become official, at least in Ian's own mind. This is why the Evangelical Alliance group of pastors in the town of Velbert were, many years later in October 2010, proud and delighted to invite my son, Mark, me, and local friends to celebrate the founding of Torchbearers in their own city. We spent the weekend among them and were treated most graciously, like VIPs. On Sunday morning, Mark preached the sermon in one of their churches. Then one evening we shared the history of Torchbearers, using a slide presentation. It was a special joy to be able to show a picture of the first group of thirty German young people who originally came to us way back in 1948. Best of all, was to have a picture of three "boys," including Eberhard Witte, who had come from Velbert with that first group, shown standing together in the courtyard at Capernwray sixty-two years earlier. Some of the men and women at the meeting had also spent time as young people at Capernwray.

The local newspaper printed an article concerning the celebrations in 2010 with the title "Major Thomas: An Officer of the Occupying Force Turned Friend." The Evangelical Alliance pastors then added to the newspaper article: "There is hardly any documentation of the military town commander Major Ian Thomas in Velbert, but much more can be said about the impact Thomas left as a Christian who soon had forged a link to Velbert Christians."

Returning back to 1948, Ian's report continued:

> **Wednesday, March 8th** *"Day in Velbert, talked to various boys."*

Ian had to make doubly sure that these new young Torchbearers realized what they had been called to do.

On Thursday, March 9, having seen God at work in Germany and little knowing how much more we would share in His work in the coming years, the itinerary simply stated: *"Leaving Velbert for England via Brussels."*

5

The Continuing Story

Many in our first group of German young people were truly enthusiastic about their new-found faith, and they requested further teaching from the Bible. With their God-given desire to lead others in their homeland to Christ, it was vital that these new believers should be given the opportunity to study God's Word for an extended time.

Ian and Mr. Van Dooren, whom our staff and children referred to as "Van" and "Uncle Van," discussed the possibilities and sought to follow God's leading, trusting Him to "direct their ways," according to Proverbs 3:5–6. Since the summer conferences were ending in early October, with one Christmas conference in December, the house was not fully in use until almost Easter. We considered that the available intervening months could provide an opportunity for a "Short-Term Bible School." So it was that the first "Capernwray Bible School" began in October 1949, lasting for six months. Van became the principal and undertook some of the teaching. He also contacted pastors, preachers, missionaries and others who were known to be evangelical and Christ-centered in doctrine who could teach basic biblical truth from God's Word. Ian was traveling in the British Isles at that time, speaking at various churches and conventions, but when at home, he also taught at the Bible school. Upon hearing about the new ministry at Capernwray, many became interested in visiting us, offering their help in various and generous ways.

Colonel Marton's old billiard room, furnished now with some desks and with chairs, soon became the Capernwray Bible School lecture hall. As far as we were able, we made efforts to inform our previous German guests and other friends and contacts about the opening of the Bible school. We kept the fees as low as possible and waited in anticipation for the first arrivals.

Van's record, kept safely in the archives, includes the following:

> It was with considerable joy and anticipation that we welcomed in October 1949, the first party of students from the Continent for the International Bible School. Others joined the school within the next few weeks until the total of students reached thirty, fourteen girls and sixteen fellows. Several nationalities were represented. The majority came from Germany and others were from Austria, one student was English and for a while there were students from Holland and Switzerland. Of those expected from Spain, only one was able to obtain the necessary permission to come and, unfortunately, did not arrive until near the end of the second term. Two students became Christians.

As we can see, the Bible school did not run perfectly. Students did not all arrive on the expected day, for example, but during the "next few weeks." However, all sat under God's Word in the classroom.

We faced a different kind of challenge when a church in Germany sent some students who were not true believers. I can well remember being somewhat shocked to discover on my rounds one evening that one fellow and one girl, who had only just met each other a few days earlier, were in a warm embrace in one of the corridors. I quickly reported this to Van, saying he needed to stop this behavior and that we must initiate some student rules. Being the bachelor that he was, Van, with a tone of embarrassment, quickly replied, "You take care of it." We certainly had a lot to learn about the smooth running of an international Bible school.

For two additional years, the British government continued to support the sending of more specially chosen German young people to spend the summer at Capernwray. Apart from these, other Germans were finding their own way, and pastors and youth leaders were also making group reservations. Ian continued to visit Torchbearers and to hold meetings in Germany, often returning to us with his Vauxhall filled with young Germans. Much as we loved them, Capernwray was almost overcome with Germans. Even the local farmers blamed "those Germans at Capernwray" when their precious stone walls dividing one field from another, had broken down because people were climbing over them. At one point, Ian almost decided that "enough is enough" when it came to German young people, but he always relented.

Starting All Over Again

Dwight Wadsworth, an American who had served in Germany as an army chaplain during World War II, had, like Ian, come to care for German youth. When the conflict ended, he and his family had moved to Glasgow, Scotland so that he could study at the university for a Ph.D. In 1952, Dwight came to Capernwray as a speaker at one of the summer conference weeks. Anticipating sharing God's Word with a group of British young people, he was somewhat surprised but delighted to arrive in the entrance hall only to be warmly welcomed by a crowd of noisy young Germans. Dwight had already begun to speak their language, and playing his guitar, he loved to lead them in singing German hymns and choruses. All of the guests, spent a great week of fellowship with Dwight's Bible teaching and his fine singing.

Happy to return the following year, Dwight was now delighted to discuss with Ian the possibility of establishing a similar Torchbearer ministry across the Channel in Germany. They decided to rent, at least for a time, a small apartment in the city of Wuppertal in the north, where some of our early German young people and Bible school students had originated. For the American Wadsworth family it meant uprooting Velma, Dwight's wife, and their young son and daughter from a temporary home in Scotland and sending them to live in a foreign land. This they did in 1954. Our good friend and secretary at Capernwray, Vera Porter, later Vera Cowie, moved there with the Wadsworths, armed with pages of names and addresses of our Germans ready to take up Torchbearer business. In addition, Rosi Berger, whom Ian had already met with her parents and family of four brothers in Hamburg, also joined Torchbearers in Wuppertal and, with Vera, managed the office work, among other duties. Rosi little knew on the day she began working there that she would continue to do so for the next thirty-nine years in many different capacities. Such is the call of God for some of His children.

Before long, the Wadsworths received many visitors to their home after young people who lived near the city began to hear word that Torchbearers had arrived. They were drawn to the Wadsworth home for Christian fellowship, further instruction in God's Word, and to join Dwight in his hearty and happy singing. Added to these were, on many occasions, British soldiers stationed in the vicinity who had already met with Dwight at Capernwray, or in other places.

Since the apartment was small, on some occasions it became necessary for part of the "congregation" either to stand or sit outside the building, praising the Lord with their loud and joyful voices. The inevitable soon happened, when elderly neighbors seeking peace and quiet began complaining about the noise coming from 93 Victoria Strasse.

It was also inevitable that Ian would one day receive a letter from Dwight saying, "I need a big house like Capernwray in a country area of Germany where we have room to develop a real Torchbearer Centre." How, though, and where?

In retrospect we can but say again, "God did it"!

A Big House in Germany

Dwight Wadsworth began a serious search for his big house so that he might develop "a real Torchbearer Centre in Germany." Ian was also continuing to spend some months each year traveling around Germany speaking in meetings, usually arranged by Torchbearers, and in churches, boarding schools, homes, and other locations. After three years, the British government had ended its sponsorship of sending young Germans to England, but we continued to accommodate those who still wished to visit either the summer conferences or winter Bible school at their own expense, though usually at a reduced fee. Frequently, some traveled with school groups led by fine Christian teachers. Others came to us through arrangements made by such organizations as the German YMCA. Ian also frequently invited individual Germans to return with him to Capernwray after his travels. He would arrive home in the Vauxhall crammed tight with German boys, having obtained from surprised but happy parents the permission to give their sons a good holiday staying at a Christian youth center in England.

Although Dwight's search for a German Capernwray had not yet brought success, God was working quietly on His plans. A young German man named Peter Arhelger from the town of Limburg had stayed at Capernwray at Ian's invitation. Following that visit, Ian came to know Peter's family, staying with them in 1957 while he held meetings in the town. At that time, Ian mentioned he had heard of a partly ruined castle named Schloss Langenau situated somewhere in the area, and that he wished to see this castle in case it might be suitable for Torchbearers. Since Peter knew the area so well, he helped Ian find the way to the castle. When driving through the nearby village of Obernhof, a policeman emerged from a pub just a little the worse for a glass or two of German beer. When Ian stopped to ask him if he knew anything about Schloss Langenau, the policeman was very happy to talk, saying it was partly ruined and that there were some refugees living in part of it. He became surprisingly in-formative, and, pointing across the nearby river, our policeman simply stated, "Across that river, Klostermühle is for rent." Peter recalled, "Ian did a U-turn and without any hesitation drove in the direction to which the talkative policeman had pointed and indeed found Klostermühle." Here he had a long talk with the proprietress, Frau Schwamm, and sometime later, Peter said, "Ian came out of the house, got into the car and said with his typical smile, 'I think we've got it!'"

Originally Klostermühle, as the name suggests, had been the mill belonging to the huge cloister on top of the hill immediately above the various buildings below. In the years until our local policeman happened to lead Ian and Peter to the place, it had been operated as a small guest house with a pub and restaurant available for locals and day hikers since it was at the end of a popular and picturesque hiking route. By the time Ian saw the place, only one of the main buildings was usable, and most of the other premises were badly neglected and dilapidated. A tremendous amount of hard work lay ahead. Despite all of this, Dwight and Velma, believing that God had indeed called them to the Torchbearer ministry in this somewhat unusual place, accepted the challenge and with their two young children and Rosi Berger, left Wuppertal and moved into Klostermühle in October 1958. Vera Cowie was now much needed back in the office at Capernwray where she would continue to serve the Lord, not only as a secretary, which was not always easy in those first challenging early years of the work, but also in personal ministry with guests and students. For me, Vera's willingness and ability to serve as a temporary "mother" to our small boys when I was able to travel on occasions with Ian, was a gift from God.

Klostermühle was built alongside a very small river valley with trees on either side, almost tucked into this little valley with its main and tallest two-story building at the far end. Although other parts of the property were clearly not usable, this main building became the place where the Wadsworth family and Rosi could live for the time being. There were fifteen bedrooms, each with its own washbasin, with just one main bathroom and two toilets. The downstairs consisted of a dining room and kitchen, while across from the front entrance there was a meeting room.

When Ian visited after they'd taken possession of the place, he was as delighted as he'd been upon first seeing Capernwray Hall. As one of a family of architects, Ian could always see the true potential in buildings, just as he did in the lives of some people he met around the world. Capernwray Hall had been opened for our first guests in 1947; now it was 1958 and we were starting all over again.

Dwight and Ian had the opportunity to inspect every corner of the property and to plan for the most immediate improvements and alterations to the buildings so that Klostermühle could, as soon as possible, be opened as the first Torchbearer Centre in Germany. As soon as word went around to some of those early Torchbearers who had visited us in Capernwray from Germany, as well as others whom Ian had met on his weeks of ministry within that country, there were offers of help. Dwight was also busy contacting and recruiting young Torchbearers as he organized Christian holidays for those who were available and interested. From these Germans with whom Dwight already had contact, he took groups to Greece, Spain, and other European countries, even to Palestine. Torchbearers were on the march. Some of these were among the early volunteers to come and support their very own Torchbearer Centre in Germany.

Ian now had to contend with matters of business in the German language. At first, our good friend and German secretary Amie Schaub became an excellent interpreter in meetings, and even taught us some German as we traveled until, in time, Ian became proficient in the language. He was delighted finally to teach and preach in the language of the people. Initially, though, matters relating to the laws of transfer of business, change of usage, part purchase or rental, and much more kept Ian at a desk long into the night.

For the first ten years of operation, Torchbearers rented most of the property so that permission for improvements and alterations needed to be sought from the owners. Dwight, Velma and Rosi were all on the job sharing many hours of their day making preparations for the time when Klostermühle, while retaining its old name, would become a second Torchbearer Centre brought into being by nothing less than an act of God.

Klostermühle opened to its first guests in 1958. Dwight Wadsworth became the director and, having been a pastor in California prior to World War II and gaining his Ph.D. in Scotland before joining Torchbearers, he was the obvious choice to become the principal of Klostermühle's first Bible school, consisting of twenty students that began for three months in January 1960.

Meanwhile, it became obvious that the Wadsworth children, Gail and Bruce, would soon have to be sent to an English-speaking school. They were learning German easily, but their parents knew that for their education to be complete, they needed to continue their studies in an English grammar school. This was no easy decision for Dwight and Velma, but it happened in obedience to the Jesus, who spoke of following Him as "taking up your cross" and dying to your own rights.

Ongoing Partnership

"Fackeltraeger," was becoming increasingly known in Germany, not only through those who had visited Capernwray Hall or had attended the Bible school, but through the establishment of their own Torchbearer Centre in the attractive Lahn Valley. Klostermühle was intended to be a place where German young folks would meet Christ, bring their friends, and experience the joy of Christian fellowship while sharing a really good holiday. This was indeed the case. The Wadsworths had already been learning the German language in Wuppertal, so Dwight could teach and preach at the Centre, as well as invite some German teachers and preachers, while Velma cooked good German meals. Rosi and one or two staff were everywhere on the job. The singing at the meetings was great too, a blend of old and new songs and hymns.

As a means of encouraging further fellowship and friendship between our two countries, an opportunity for British young folks to visit Klostermuhle was now given in a printed brochure that we mailed to all those British folks who had attended Capernwray summer conferences. There were now many, since we had been in business for almost twelve years. In 1959, the total cost, according to the brochure, for travel from London, the two-week stay at the Centre and one full day excursion was just UK £18! A leader from Capernwray accompanied the group, and I believe those visits were blessed and enjoyed, while friendship between the two nationalities continued to develop. We made those opportunities available for several years.

6

Growth at Capernwray

Meanwhile, the number of guests attending the summer conferences at Capernwray Hall gradually increased. We had a fine problem on our hands. Had not God promised His great goodness was "stored up" ready for us? (see Ps. 31:19) Ian had wanted a "big house somewhere," and got it! But it was not big enough. Those twenty-one bedrooms, with the three more much smaller ones on the second floor, became inadequate for the growing numbers of guests wishing to spend a week's vacation with us. Not only did they come from the British Isles, but continuing numbers of people—families, teenagers, young and older people—now came from other countries.

What could be done about the problem? Born into a family of architects, Ian saw that the stables around the old courtyard could be converted. Lowering the floors of the haylofts, installing windows and stairways, and decorating the walls provided accommodation for a number of young men, though they were rather unsuitable for girls. For a time, those young men had to go to bed by ladder and so enter their dormitory through a round window in the stone wall of the second floor used originally for throwing the hay out to the courtyard to feed the Marton's fine horses.

We also, for a time, made use of the small family church on the property as a temporary dormitory, just a few minutes distance from the main house. The original old oak pews had already been removed due to dry rot, and to give more accommodation we installed a second floor, giving space for forty beds in all. Some German boys were coming to Capernwray in groups, others with one or two friends, but all were glad to have a bed in the "church" and to pay at a greatly reduced rate for their stay. They could still take part in all the activities, meals and meetings at the main house. One young leader named Bernhard Rebsch, from Berlin, delighted those sometimes hungry boys by bringing trays of leftover sandwiches and bread at bedtime from the main house. Bernhard was a true believer and a caring leader, so much so that many years later he became a much loved and effective director at Klostermühle.

Another need developed for space in the former Marton's dining room, which had become our conference hall. It had seemed so large at first, but as it filled with rows of chairs, the big room with its high ceiling and huge fireplace became totally inadequate. Fortunately, between this room and the lounge there was a fairly wide connecting door, which was kept open during meetings. Chairs were placed at and beyond this open door to the opposite end of the lounge in order to accommodate those guests who found no seating in the main meeting hall. Although a somewhat primitive "loud speaker" system was used, it wasn't efficient. Direct translation of the messages was given from a side room for our German guests by German staff and leaders, but that was not by any means satisfactory.

There were many inconveniences in those early days at Capernwray. Staff worked long hours, and sometimes there were not enough of them. Guests were not always happy with their accommodations, and the German boys were always hungry. Meals had to be brought from the kitchen along stone-flagged corridors to three different dining rooms, since no one single room was big enough to seat about 150 or more people. Throughout the house there were constant repairs needing to be done, and when rain was heavy, the roof leaked onto the main carpeted stairs. In addition, there were times when the accounts in the office did not always balance.

Despite these and other matters, there was a sense of joy, of fulfillment and purpose, and that spirit of fellowship only to be found together in Christ. God was here and, by His presence, lives were being blessed and changed forever. For some of our guests, life would never be the same again since they had received a new life—eternal life, Christ Himself. Even before our eyes, Ian's passion, as he wrote to me during World War II, was being fulfilled: "I have seen more clearly than ever the complete emptiness of a life, apart from the single purpose of bringing men, women and children to Christ—a purpose around which every activity and circumstance must revolve. Hallelujah."

Changed Lives

A testimony from a young German girl at that time is typical of the many whose lives were changed forever after their visit to our big house where God still lives and continues to seek and save the lost. Marlies Vermillion, then a German teenager, now a grandmother and living in the United States, wrote: "I was raised in a nominal Christian home. Christianity seemed to be a lot of things I wasn't supposed to do. I had come to the place where I didn't think it was worthwhile and was ready to give up. In 1953 I was invited to a meeting in my cousin's home where an English major was to speak. He invited us to Capernwray for our summer vacation. I thought a trip to England might help with my English. There, for the first time ever, I heard that I cannot live the Christian life, that it is not a set of rules but a relationship, and that only the Lord Jesus Himself must live that life through me. Understanding my part in this relationship, I came back from England a changed person so that today, over fifty years later, I can say I have experienced the presence of the Lord in all life's ups and downs. I am so grateful for the life-changing message that Torchbearers still teaches."

The winter Bible school at Capernwray was drawing more students from around the world and continuing to be in the able hands of "Van" who, on many occasions, also led the summer conference weeks. Ian was now available to speak at Bible conferences and to teach God's Word in church fellowships overseas. On one occasion he was invited to visit New Zealand and among other meetings, he spoke at the Ngaruawahia Easter Convention. Following one of the meetings, a young man named Haldane Rowan came to speak with Ian. Haldane wrote: "I was at the Ngaruawahia Convention where Major was speaking. After one meeting, I went up to him to thank him because the Lord had spoken to me. Major asked me what I did. 'I'm a plumber.' He invited me to England. The rest is 'His Story.'"

God's story brought about the arrival of Haldane and his wife, Thelma, recently married, as they traveled from the other side of the world to Capernwray. We faced a dilemma concerning the need for a bigger meeting hall, and to our delight, Haldane we soon discovered, was more than a plumber—he also had building skills. Along with the help of a team of strong and willing young men, we watched an attractive meeting hall being built at the far end of the large rose garden, close enough to the main buildings, with a view of the parkland and large enough to seat at least two hundred people, even more if needed. At either side of the raised platform, translation booths were built so that with the latest technology at the time, our translators could sit, listen through headphones, and translate the messages for those who needed to hear in their own language, and could do so through individual headsets.

Due to the slope of this part of the gardens, it was possible to build a number of dormitories and bathrooms below the meeting hall. We forfeited a few flower beds, as well as the end wall of the rose garden, but what was that as we watched the much-needed building being constructed? It was my joy to notice that Haldane and his team always prayed outside the building every morning before they commenced work.

God knew our dilemmas at Capernwray long before we did. As Jesus said in Matthew 6:8, "Your Father knows what you need before you ask him." He also knew a preacher willing to leave home and travel many miles to talk about His Son, our Lord Jesus, and a plumber and his wife, who were willing to leave the easy life at home to embark on a long journey for Christ's sake, without knowing any conditions at the other end.

Easter came, when the Hall with the dormitories below needed to be ready to receive a large group of young people for a teenager conference. Haldane, having worked the whole of the previous day, worked all night long in order to complete painting the bedroom ceilings. He finally arrived for staff lunch next day. When a girl placed a bowl of soup at his place at the table and Haldane bowed his head to give thanks, he fell asleep with his nose in the soup.

Within the walls of the Capernwray Conference Hall, the Lord has spoken to hundreds of people, men, women and children from many nations, just as He spoke to Haldane at that conference in New Zealand. May He continue to speak through the ministry of Torchbearers and through all those to whom He is truly Savior and Lord.

The Significance of the Insignificant

As the ministry of Torchbearing has progressed over many years, I have noticed frequently how God in His wisdom and foreknowledge has used insignificant situations, small "happenings" and seemingly unimportant people to fulfill His plans and purposes. We read in God's Word about small things and individuals who were extremely important to Him and to His plans—just a shepherd boy, young David, who became a king for God's people and whose earthly lineage is in that of our Lord Jesus. Also, an unnamed boy with whose lunch Jesus fed a multitude. God needed and found in Esther a young woman prepared to risk her life so that His future purposes could be fulfilled. There are many more similar examples in Scripture.

For us, Torchbearers began in the heart of God in eternity past, but on earth He began with a boy of thirteen who had a desire for a neighbor friend of twelve to come to know his Savior, Jesus, whom he had received personally at a Christian camp for boys just like himself. Then this friend and neighbor, Ian Thomas, having come quietly in his heart to receive a brand new life in Christ, grew up to become an evangelist. At the outbreak of World War II, he became a soldier but he retained such a passion for leading people to Christ that he was willing, when the war was over, to spend his small amount of savings in order to purchase a huge old house for the sole purpose of sharing

Christ with others. I happened to be the evangelist's inexperienced young wife, with no knowledge of auctions nor business deals, but somehow was prompted to risk that final bid of "just a little further" for such a house, in order to satisfy the wishes of, as I thought at the time, my crazy husband.

Writing in First Corinthians 1:26–28, the Apostle Paul describes the kind of people God calls to His service: "not many wise men . . . not many mighty, not many noble" (KJV), and "God also selected (deliberately chose) what in the world is lowborn *and* insignificant" (AMP). The reason God does so is clearly expressed in verse 29: "So that no mortal man should [have pretense for glorying and] boast in the presence of God" (AMP). In other words, we may indeed say "God did it," and we may agree with James in his book, "Humble yourselves [feeling very insignificant] in the presence of the Lord, and He will exalt you [He will lift you up and make your lives significant]" (4:10, AMP). In response to the obedience of faith, God delights to use us where He chooses, in His service.

Looking back on the developing growth of Torchbearers, now worldwide, we have come to realize that frequently God used normal and common situations to fulfill His purposes. Traveling in post-war Germany, it was normal, for instance, for us to pick up hitchhikers, of which there were many waiting for us along Germany's roadsides. On Friday, June 19, 1953, in the familiar old Vauxhall with Rosi Berger, her brother Hans, a recently-invited hitchhiker already filling the back seat, with ourselves in the front of the car, we were on our way to the town of Bad Godesberg where Ian was to speak at an evening meeting. We passed a tall German boy requesting a ride. The car being full, Ian drove on until he felt strangely moved to drive back and pick him up. Peter Wiegand, who soon made his name known to us, in accounting his experience many years later, wrote, "You invited me into an already much overloaded Vauxhall, and squeezed me into the gap between the front seats." Ian then drove on, while the Bergers soon began, in German of course, to explain what our journey was about and, keen Torchbearers that they were, how Peter could be saved. Soon it was time to stop and share our German rolls with everyone in the car which, as Peter later explained, made a very good impression on him. We drove on to our destination, arriving at the home where we had been invited to stay overnight and where our hostess found room for Peter to stay also. This meant that he too attended the meeting which had been planned. He recounted later that following the meeting and on returning to the home, "The Major led me to the Lord; it was after midnight in the very early hours of Saturday, June 20th 1953. It seems like yesterday and still touches me with awe and wonder, gratitude and utter surprise."

Peter's home was in Hamburg, where Ian visited a year later, and Peter recorded that in the following years, "Each one in our family accepted Christ." It was then in 1958 that our grateful and excited hitchhiker came to Capernwray to assist with the continental groups of young folks and, having left his job in Germany, he attended the Capernwray Bible School. Later, Peter studied at the Bible Institute in Glasgow, Scotland, for two years while using his available holidays to "help the Major with his correspondence." During the time Peter Wiegand was working at Capernwray, a delightful German girl called Runhild was also assisting on staff, having come to Christ at Major's meetings in her hometown of Aurich. We noticed a friendship developing even as the two walked along the old stone flagged corridors on their way to staff meals. Their marriage took place in Aurich in 1962.

By this time at Capernwray Hall, the number of guests for the summer conferences was increasing, and there were numbers of students enrolling for the winter Bible schools. A little magazine entitled *Torch* had been issued earlier with news of the expanding ministry worldwide, which included copies of encouraging letters we had received from some of the Germans who had attended the Bible school. About this time, too, it was announced in the *Torch* magazine that The Capernwray Missionary Trust Fund had been established and fully recognized by the tax authorities as a charity for income tax purposes. This enabled friends of Torchbearers to support financially those attending winter Bible school, in particular some of the German young folk who had recently become Christians.

Here God used one of those apparently "insignificant happenings" to undergird His work with unexpected significance. My sister, Mary, had helped in working at Capernwray Hall when we first moved into the building back in 1946, and in early 1947 she "happened" to have a friend who needed a holiday. It was not easy to find comfortable hotels so soon after the war, and Mary recommended Capernwray. This friend had for some time been seeking a way to find God and doing so by investigating various cults and religions, but without an answer to her need. She had made a reservation for three weeks at Capernwray and was somewhat surprised to discover that she was expected to attend two meetings daily. Not only that, but those who preached spoke often about a second coming of Christ of which she had never heard. At the same time, some of the other guests kept talking to her about conversion and being saved. Despite having heard the gospel clearly explained, we had to assume that our friend had returned home in the same condition as she came, not having made any visible response to what she had heard. However, we soon received a letter saying, "When I came home, you may be surprised to know that I did what you told me at the meetings at Capernwray and I received Christ. What do I do now?" That brief note was a great reason for a time of joyful praising by the staff at Capernwray. It also gave me every reason to have whispered those words, "just go a little further," at the auction for Capernwray Hall less than a year earlier. Now, of course, our dear friend could not keep away, visiting time and time again over many years. She constantly served her Savior by opening her small home to students and to many others needing a place to share fellowship together over the cups of tea or coffee she provided for them, and often more than that. In her later years, Mary's friend was cared for in her own house by a very good and competent person until she was finally taken to her home in heaven.

The significance of this, my true story, is in demonstration of the truth mentioned at the beginning of this chapter, that God sometimes uses small, seemingly unimportant "happenings" in order to fulfill His plans and purposes.

As I mentioned, Torchbearers had established a trust fund so that donors could enable us to enroll students in the Bible School from countries overseas for whom it would otherwise be financially impossible to attend. When Mary's friend, who simply "happened" to visit Capernwray and finally found a loving God for whom she had searched, died, her will stated that she had left funds in the form of shares to eight different missionary groups at home and overseas which she had delighted to support after she had come to know our Lord for herself. As an only child, our good friend had inherited an amount of stocks and shares which, instead of using solely for her own purposes, such as purchasing a larger home for herself which she could well have preferred, she found far greater satisfaction in knowing that her missionary friends at home and abroad would be blessed and encouraged in their ministry when to their joy the funds would be made available to them. At the same time, much needed income for the Torchbearers Trust Fund was generously provided.

There came a day when I was talking with a student from Romania in the hallway at Capernwray, and he asked me how he could possibly attend the Bible School without having the necessary fees. I told him the story of our special friend, a lady whose name never "hit the headlines," and who lived on a street in a small house, but who came to know and love Jesus so much that she wanted to share Him with many others around the world. I saw tears of gratitude on the cheeks of the Romanian student as we talked. The year that I spoke with him "happened" to coincide with the tearing down of the Berlin Wall. We were indeed blessed, since it was possible to receive twelve students that very year from East Germany, Albania, Russia, and other former Communist countries so that they could return home to share Christ and His Word with friends and family. The funds we received then have been carefully and professionally invested, and still continue to bring blessing, not only now to East Europeans, but also to Africans, Indians and many others. As they study what God has to say in His life-changing book at Torchbearers Bible Schools so, we trust, they will become more effective in leading others to Christ.

I am glad that my sister Mary once "had a friend," and that this friend needed a holiday. Such was the insignificant happening which even now continues to bring significance to people from many countries who wish to know more about a God who changes lives.

Happenings at the Hall

Capernwray was constantly a busy place—things were always happening. Outside staff would be mowing lawns, weeding or planting the gardens, building and much else beside. The guests might be playing tennis or croquet, having a "dip" in the swimming pool, or it might be meeting time. The bookshop could be open, or even the "Beehive," a snack bar, which in the time of the Marton family was a horse stable in the courtyard, but which Ian used to describe as a place "where sweet things are sold by sweet things!" Of course, he knew the Beehive was just one of my responsibilities.

Staff indoors would be cooking or laying tables for the next meal, or maybe still washing up from the last one. We did indeed have a so-called "wooden washing-up machine" in the old days, but it washed but one cup at a time between rotating brushes—the plates likewise. The office staff was always answering the one phone in the whole building, so the only way to find staff and guests to take a phone call was to run around those stone flagged corridors shouting. They typed every letter—no computers or copying machines just a piece of copy paper between sheets of paper.

A number of years ago, when Bible school finished in mid-March, there followed the Easter teenager weeks. Christian teachers from schools in many parts of the country would bring groups of those they taught at school, for a week at Capernwray. Their young people were expected to attend morning and evening meetings, just like the adult weeks. The gospel would be clearly explained in the meetings and in private conversations. In fact, all the Capernwray staff who were available were assigned a dormitory where they were to lead short devotions before breakfast each morning, and again in the evenings at bedtime. We were called "Room Officers." When possible, we tried to spend other times with "our" young folks and come to know them. We were even invited at times to their permitted "midnight feasts" on the last night of the week in the dorms. These were truly "all day" working days, but wonderful times of blessing.

Using bunk beds, it was possible at that time to accommodate up to almost two hundred teenagers each week. There was plenty of opportunity for fun and games, and for enjoying trips by bus or car. Though many of the children came from totally godless, unchurched homes, some of these youngsters, during their stay, put their trust in Christ and returned to Capernwray often. I remember on one occasion on Saturday night going to my assigned room number twelve to meet eight girls from the city of Liverpool. On the walls of that newly painted room, they had stuck huge paper figures of young men, though older than they, and pictured with guitars and obviously singing. Taken aback, I asked who they were. The answer came loud and clear and in a strong Liverpool dialect: "The Beatles, Miss!" At that time I had not heard of these men, so I replied that we did not want beetles at Capernwray, but soon all was explained to me by a chorus of eight voices. It was not easy to read a verse of Scripture and pray after that.

After that Easter week for teenagers each year, there followed a second week, usually for older youths, and it was also a joy to see some responding to the claims of Christ, and others growing in Him. On Friday nights, we normally included a testimony time, as in the adult weeks. On one occasion, a young man about eighteen years of age and in his last year of school gave testimony. He had come that week as an atheist, having no belief in God as creator and denying anything he heard about the Lord Jesus, all of which his teacher at school had taught him. At Capernwray, his Room Officer "just happened" to be a fully qualified biology and science teacher and a true believer in Jesus Christ. Who better to be his Room Officer? That student came to receive the Lord Jesus into his life that week and went away rejoicing in his newly found believing faith in the Creator Redeemer. Following teenager weeks, there was always much cleaning to be done, as an adult Easter conference would be scheduled almost immediately.

The winter Bible school had been in operation for a few years when Stuart Briscoe and his wife, Jill, came on staff, full of enthusiasm for the ministry of Torchbearing. Jill asked one day, "Where is your youth work?" We explained it was right here in Capernwray for several weeks in very early spring. "No, I mean in town." Jill was not satisfied with "right here." She looked beyond to teenagers who might never come to a place like Capernwray. So in a very short time, she had "borrowed" an old barn from a local farmer, filled it with kids from the locality, and begun a work which has borne spiritual fruit for many years all over our area and beyond. One day someone must write a book about what happened in answer to her simple question.

Meanwhile, Stuart was also thinking. He asked us, "Folks don't usually come to holiday conferences in early spring—that's why we have too many empty beds! Why not add a spring term to the winter Bible school?" It was agreed. Now, having Torchbearer Bible Schools elsewhere, students may spend two terms at Capernwray and a third term in Tauernhof, Austria, or Sweden, or maybe after New Zealand or Australia, they can come to follow up with a term in Europe.

A key member of our staff in those years was a man from Scotland named Billy Strachan. Billy had known a sad home life, his mother having died when he was just nine years old and his dad, owning a pub, made the boy sell drink from an early age. It was not until he joined the army that Billy heard the gospel from a chaplain who led him to Christ. Ian was asked to speak to the men at Billy's army unit and invited him to Capernwray. Billy Strachan, with his God-given gifts of fun and magic, could captivate our teenagers, who discovered that they could have fun and still be Christians. Even some of my Liverpool girls in Room Twelve came to Christ that week. Billy Strachan spent two years at a Bible school in the United States, returned to Capernwray, married Grace, by now the secretary in our office, and later, following the retirement of "Uncle Van," Billy became the principal of the Capernwray Bible School. He was absolutely down to earth in his teaching and entirely biblical. He followed up students by his letters, and some continue to listen to him by tape. Very suddenly, after a week of teaching at Tauernhof Bible School, God took Billy home to Himself.

Ian met Charles Price, just a boy of twelve at that time and from a family of six, in the south of England. He attended one of Ian's meetings at a local farmhouse and, as Charles says, "I was so taken with the vibrancy of the message I went back every night!" Ian noticed how attentively he listened. Charles had come to know Christ six months earlier. Charles' father was a farm worker, and the family of six with two grandmothers lived in a small two-bedroom cottage by a stream. Charles came to a "Teenagers at School" week at Capernwray, then worked on staff in the grounds and garden, farmed in Zimbabwe for two years, attended the Bible Training Institute in Scotland, and in the course of time, joined the staff at Capernwray Hall, where he met his wife. Originally just a small boy, Charles became a fine preacher and teacher, and eventually the principal of Capernwray Bible School for nine years. Now he is pastor of a church with attendance of over four thousand people in Toronto, Canada, and he can be heard on radio in many parts of the world. No wonder James writes in his letter to the dispersed Gentiles about being humble, feeling very insignificant in the presence of the Lord. He will make your lives significant. You will be able to say, "He did it." Just ask Charles!

Robert Whittaker is the current principal, and his spiritual journey in coming to Christ was a direct result of Jill Briscoe's question about our local youth work and the borrowing of a farmer's barn. Robert was a "local" who found Christ through that ministry.

Encouraging His Men

Bible school and conferences in all the Torchbearer Centres kept everyone busy looking after guests and students, while improvements to the buildings and grounds often continued at the same time. When Major Thomas was in the army and received the "Distinguished Service Order" award, part of the citation read that "he was everywhere to be found, encouraging his men. . . ." This was still the case as Torchbearers grew around the world, and with much energy and enthusiasm with the joy of the Lord in his heart, he endeavored to keep involved in all aspects of the growing ministry. He also continued as before to speak in churches, at conventions, and conferences in many places in the British Isles, and often in Germany, and elsewhere in Europe. When away from home, Ian continued to keep in touch. He expected to receive regular accounts from each centre, and dealt as best he could with problems and needs of various kinds. Even I got in trouble at times for overspending! My friend, Irene, a coworker with me at Capernwray for many years, used on occasions purchase, along with myself, items that we thought would improve the appearance of rooms—curtains, maybe new table mats, etc. In the accounts, we entered them as "sundries." When Ian received those accounts, he always needed to know what was meant by sundries—were they really essential?

It was interesting that Capernwray slowly became a meeting place for many kinds of people from many different nations and yet there was the obvious unity only to be found in Christ. We were pleased when Corrie ten Boom stayed with us at Capernwray on a couple of occasions. She was glad to have an opportunity to meet and renew an understanding with German young people in the context and atmosphere of a Christian home. The well-known British missionary to China, Gladys Aylward, also visited on occasions and enthralled us with her experiences. Ian's good friend, Dr. Alan Redpath, came with his wife Marjorie to live in a home on the grounds at Capernwray. They were with us for twelve years. Marjorie was not only an ever-willing hostess but a skilled secretary who typed many of her husband's books and letters. Dr. Redpath's ministry was of great blessing to everyone, and our Bible school students in particular will never forget sitting on the floor of the Redpath's lounge around Alan's big armchair as he answered their questions, teaching them from God's Word and sharing his love for Jesus Christ.

7

Europe Welcomes More Torchbearers

When we welcomed our very first visitors in May 1947, and even when the name "Torchbearers" was heard in Germany as early as 1948, only God could know just how far that "Torch" would share its light around the world. From Germany to Austria, to nearby Switzerland and, at the "last count," to seven other European countries, Torchbearer Centres have been established. From the Centres themselves, many individuals, including those who have attended either Torchbearer Bible schools or holiday conferences, have carried the torch of life and light back home. For some it has been back to the workplace, and for others to a missionary assignment or working with a youth group, or perhaps simply to attend college or to live with folks at home. Every Christian has opportunities, not only to speak God's truth as understood from within His Word, but also to "show and tell" that truth about the living Word, our Lord Jesus. Whoever we may be, there is to be seen in our lives the fact that the Lord Jesus died for us to give Himself to us and to live that life through us. That was the message that ushered Ian into full-time Christian ministry at the age of nineteen, first to his own country, and then through the "Missionary Fellowship of Torchbearers" around the world.

At first, as we have seen, God gave opportunities in the British Isles, then in Germany and Austria. Staff, led by Peter Wiegand at Schloss Klaus, saw many other opportunities to serve and share the life and light of Jesus Christ outside Austria by sending spiritual and practical help, even as far as Ethiopia, Micronesia, India, the Sudan and elsewhere. In their local town, they also established a ministry in two care centers and a home exclusively for the benefit of the handicapped, a work still continuing to bear much spiritual fruit. No wonder Ian was once prompted to reverse down a German highway and to squeeze a certain hitchhiker into the space between the front seats.

My Childhood Dream Come True

As a child in our small house in Belfast, Northern Ireland, I used to gaze with wonder at a particular picture which hung on the wall of our dining room. It showed a small girl about my size sitting alone in an absolute sea of multi-colored wild flowers in what I discovered later to be the famous Tyrol, a province of beautiful Austria. It became a childish dream of mine to be that little girl surrounded on all sides by such flowers on some sunny day, with blue sky overhead and no one around to call me away. Many years went by before that dream came true, but when it did, God Himself brought that, and dreams that I never even dreamt, to reality.

For some time at Capernwray those of us who lived and worked had the amazing experience of coming to care for and love our German young people, but it was not until Ian received

Ian Thomas at nineteen

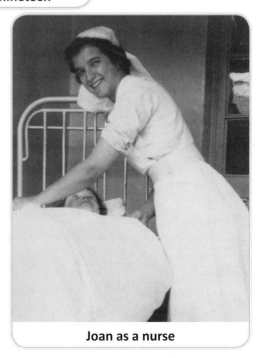

Joan as a nurse

Major Thomas in uniform

Ian and Joan's wedding

Nottingham Home with Joan and Chris in the garden

Letters between Ian and Joan

Ian's Bible

Private houses supposed to be suitable for officers' billets

Number	Name of house-owner	Street
1	Karl Berninghaus	39, Hoferstrasse ✓
2	Emil Engstfeld	5, Kempstrasse ✓
3	Otto Fliether	161, Heidestrasse ✓
4	Jakob Hammel	57, Hedderstrasse ✓
5	Karl Hassiepen	7, Hommerstrasse
6	Edmund Hegenberg	9, Lindenstrasse
7	Walter Helkenberg	23, Offerstrasse ✓
8	Ernst Hülsbeck	5, Sommerstrasse ✓
9	Friedrich Jüngst	94, Hindenburgstrasse
10	Ernst Inkenhaus	13, Schillerstrasse
11	Paul Oesthaus	18, Südstrasse
12	Edmund Schaaf	4, Schillerstrasse ✓
13	Max Schulte	34, Kirchstrasse ✓
14	Sittel - Bohle	39, Blumenstrasse ✓
15	W. Vallcuer	42, Blumenstrasse ✓
16	Ernst Vossinkel	299, Friedrichstrasse ✓
17	Albert Voss	42, Hohenzollernstrasse ✓
18	Alfred Wenke	21, Bismarckstrasse ✓
19	Albert Weyermann	84, Hindenburgstrasse ✓
20	Hans Witte	

Velbert, August 9th, 1945
Schu/Kr

F = List of German homes used by soldiers (attached)

List of homes used by soldiers

LOT I
(Coloured Red on Plan).

The Attractive and Very Substantially Built

COUNTRY MANSION

known as

Capernwray Hall

of medium size, occupying a slightly elevated site amidst its own grounds with stately forest trees and overlooking a well-timbered park. It is approached by two winding carriage drives, in a good state of repair, guarded by

TWO ENTRANCE LODGES
(One Lodge is occupied on a Service Tenancy), both built of stone and slated.

THE MANSION
comprises:—
LOFTY AND SPACIOUS HALL
fitted stone fireplace and Dog Grate.

LIBRARY (41 ft. by 6 ins. 24 ft. 3 ins.)
with two large square Bay Windows.

DINING ROOM (36 ft. by 24 ft. 6 ins.)
with square Bay Window and Ornamental Black Marble Fireplace.

DRAWING ROOM (34 ft. by 18 ft. 3 ins.)
fitted two fine Mahogany Panelled Doors.

BILLIARDS ROOM (28 ft. by 17 ft. 9 ins.)

THE STUDY (17 ft. by 15 ft. 9 ins.)
fitted with very interesting old Oak Panelling.

CLOAK ROOM
with Lav. Basin (h. and c.) and separate w.c.

The First Floor
approached from the Hall by the Principal Staircase affords access to:—

TWENTY-ONE BEDROOMS,
Three Bathrooms, Four w.c's., Dressing-room, Linen-room.

The Second Floor
THREE BEDROOMS,
Bathroom (h. and c.). etc.

THE DOMESTIC OFFICES
are ample and sufficient for all requirements.

— 7 —

Auctioneer's brochure for Capernwray Hall

Capernwray Hall

Entry hall and staircase

Clock tower with Ian at the top repairing clock

Lounge

CAPERNWRAY.

| Mr G.B.K. Marton. Miss Phipps. | Miss L. Paffs. Hon. Mrs W. Flower. Hon. & Revd A. Phipps. | Captain Neave. | Miss Marton. Hon. Mrs G. Marton. Lt. Major Phipps. |

The Marton family

Ian and Van Dooren

Ian, Van Dooren, Eberhard Witte and friends

A Holiday Centre
for
Young Christians

Capernwray Hall

near

Morecambe Bay and England's Lovely Lakeland

Prospectus 1947

Director :
MAJOR W. IAN THOMAS, D.S.O.

Musical Director :
REV. GEOFFREY LESTER, M.A.

Secretary :
MAJOR A. GORDON GREENWOOD, A.C.A.

Telephone—CARNFORTH 185.

Capernwray Hall Prospectus

Guests in the lounge

The Thomas family

The Vauxhall with Ian, Joan and Eberhard Witte

Van Dooren and early Bible school

Klostermühle in 1957

Klostermühle today

Schloss Klaus in 1963

Schloss Klaus today

Tauernhof in 1964

Tauernhof today

The Thomas family

Capernwray Harbor

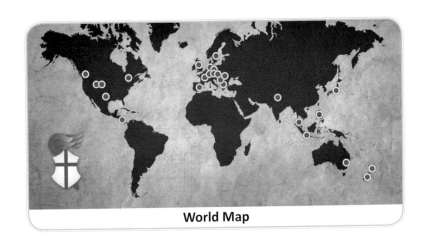

World Map

Staff photo, 2009

an invitation to minister in Austria that Austrians began to find their way to us. Driving into Austria with Ian to a town in the region of Tyrol in order to reach the address of the pastor who had invited us, I began to see wild flowers, huge areas of them, just like our picture at home. Ian kindly stopped the car, and knowing that I should not walk into the field, I leaned against the fence and with a few tears of joy, gave thanks for that old childish dream now come gloriously true.

As a result of further contacts in Austria, we were able to invite more Austrian young people to come and stay for summer Bible weeks. Some came to know Christ for themselves. In Austria on one occasion we had car trouble when the brakes failed on the vehicle which we had been loaned to drive on this particular journey, and whose owner was with us. Fortunately, we managed to arrive safely at the town of Schladming, where we needed to stay overnight for repairs. This enabled us to meet a family by the name of Kunzelmann, of whom we had already heard, who were living in a small mountain home. It was delightful to share fellowship around the table as we sang hymns and shared their food under the oil lamp hanging from the ceiling. They managed somehow to have us stay overnight. Gernot was the youngest son of eight children. He was going to leave school at the age of fourteen in order to help support the family. Ian offered to take Gernot back with us to Capernwray for a three-week visit. Little did we know that he would stay for three-and-a-half years and would one day become the director of a Torchbearer Centre in Austria.

Austria: Schloss Klaus and Tauernhof

Meanwhile, our former hitchhiker, Peter Wiegand, was still spending the summers working at Capernwray, now having the joy of meeting Austrians and with the privilege of leading a number of them to the Lord. "Somehow," as Peter described it, "my heart got bonded to them so that whenever ideas and dreams concerning ministry in Austria were verbalized, it felt like it was being addressed to me." After visiting and assisting in ministry with a strong Torchbearer group in Hamburg, Peter then followed up some of the Austrian young people. Although he had other opportunities for youth ministry, Peter accepted the invitation to settle in Austria as a full-time staff worker for Torchbearers. A small flat was found, his wife Runhild soon joined him, and their ministry quickly opened up in Schladming with youth groups, Sunday school classes and religious teaching in schools. Some boys and girls, young men and women accepted Christ, many of whom later became staff in the Torchbearer ministry as it developed.

Within a short time, Peter received information from a colleague in church youth ministry in another town about a certain noble lady in Upper Austria who owned a castle. He heard that this lady was concerned to "make it available on a lease basis for a good Christian purpose," and Peter could obtain further information by visiting a local pastor. At first, Peter was not interested since the work in Schladming was just starting and bearing spiritual fruit. Thoughts of opening a Torchbearer Centre in Schladming had even been discussed with a teacher there who had come to Christ at Capernwray and who shared that dream. However, Peter felt that they should at least see the castle for themselves. They did so, discovering a huge, partly ruined, very ancient building on a mountain overlooking the valley of Klaus, and dating back to the year 1170. The owner was a widowed heiress who took possession of her property in 1956, by which time the buildings were in very poor shape, thus she was looking for an organization to make some use of it. Due to this lady's connections to Christian noble families, she explained her wish that her property be used for a "good Christian purpose."

Ian, on seeing the building with Peter, made a satisfactory arrangement with the lady that in lieu of rent, Torchbearers would attempt a program of restoration for the castle, at least to renovate enough of the old buildings to accommodate some of our Torchbearer groups. Years earlier, the builders of the newer part of the castle had already engraved the foundation stone with the prayer, "May God Graciously Keep This House." That prayer began to be answered when, after days and weeks of very strenuous and mostly voluntary hard labor, those ancient doors were opened on July 11, 1964, to welcome the first Austrian Torchbearer Centre. A British group of forty-five guests, under the leadership of our own Stuart Briscoe, were the first to participate in a program there. God had fulfilled His own plan for Torchbearers in Austria, and it was a lot bigger than my field of flowers. He had planned that not only might I see a real field of flowers in the Tyrol, but that on occasions, I would sleep in a very ancient and truly authentic Austrian castle.

While all the negotiations for an old castle were taking place in Austria, something really new happened at Capernwray—God gave us the gift of another son. Timothy Andrew was born in the local hospital, the fourth son of our family. Little did we know then how important he would become to the ministry of Capernwray. With the title of Project Manager, he has worked, along with his team, on the old buildings. As an enthusiastic leader of groups of students and local young men on "outreach," they have brought the gospel on short-term mission trips to countries in Africa by teaching in schools, playing sports and by other means. For some years, Andy has also used his love of soccer to bring teams of players to a town in France, a spiritually needy country, where the French players, standing at the goal posts after the game or sharing in other ways, have the opportunity to understand what is involved in becoming a true Christian. On one occasion, a French player asked, "Who is that Jesus you are talking about? I never heard of him."

Remember Gernot? He was the Austrian boy who came back with us to Capernwray for three weeks and stayed for three-and-a-half years. Naturally, we added him to our family of boys and enrolled him in a local school where he received some very good reports. But he, above everything, truly excelled in sports, perhaps because from his home, Gernot had skied down a mountain to get to school every morning and trudged back up the mountain after school. We were happy to have Gernot's parents visit him at Capernwray, and in the summer holidays, he usually spent time in Austria. Having lived with our family for those years, Gernot then decided to visit his brother in Toronto, Canada, where he soon found a job. To our greatest delight, however, he later wrote to us to say he wished to attend a Bible college in Canada. Following three years of study there, it was then time to return back home to Schladming to marry his childhood sweetheart, Gertrud Vitzthum.

By one of God's "happenings," Gernot had arrived home in Schladming just as Peter Wiegand, busy as he was at Schloss Klaus, was also seeking to make arrangements to lease a former orphanage belonging to the Lutheran Church. At that time unused, it became available and could possibly be converted to a Torchbearer Centre in Schladming. When Gernot and his wife arrived, "God had," as Peter explained, "everything arranged waiting for them!" They had already accepted the invitation of Major to take over the ministry among the young people in

Schladming, plus the former orphanage, which Gernot named "Tauernhof," just at the time when we had to concentrate all our energies upon the new task at Schloss Klaus. Gernot began a very tedious job of renovation and adaptation.

Tauernhof opened as an International Centre for Torchbearers in the summer of 1966. Sportsman that he was, Gernot and his wife, Gertrud, made Tauernhof into a most attractive youth Centre, so that sports of every kind, especially skiing, became available, in addition to the summer conferences and a winter Bible school.

Added to His plans for me to smell the flowers and to sleep in a real castle, God had given me the possibility to ski, should I ever wish to do so, at no cost, whenever I visited Austria—there was an excellent ski slope right alongside Tauernhof.

Romania: Purtătorii de Făclie

In 1990, the first year after Romania gained freedom from Communism, a group of young children from that country attended a confirmation retreat at Schloss Klaus. The German pastor, Hans Dieter Krauss, accompanied these children, along with his wife, Bettina. As a result, a partnership developed between Schloss Klaus and the German Lutheran Church in Brasov, Romania. In 1997, Schloss Klaus sent Eberhard and Elke Beck to Romania. Eberhard had served at Tauernhof, and Elke happened to have attended the Torchbearer Bible School at Ravencrest in Colorado, so that as a result of these connections, there is now a Torchbearer Centre in a newly-developed area just outside the town of Brasov, Romania. "Ebbe" and Elke, along with their three children, lived in an apartment in the town and, with a small staff, worked with Romanian young people until land became available to build a Torchbearer Centre just outside the city. I had the greatest possible joy to visit Romania when the building was occurring, and about twenty happy young Christians were preparing small tents on the grounds for ninety Romanian children, due to arrive for camp the following day. There were big welcome signs everywhere. Since that time, a main building has been completed, and there are good sporting opportunities at the Centre, including a ropes course. Following the Communist years in Romania, it is now the greatest blessing that Torchbearers are free to share Christ with the people of that country.

A small river runs at the front of the Torchbearer property through which we had to drive. Now the staff has built a concrete bridge so those who come to stay have a safe way to cross over and to arrive at their destination. Perhaps that can be an illustration of crossing into the Christian life by Christ's cross. In coming years, may many folk meet with Himat Torchbearers Romania.

Albania: Crossroads

Not only in the former Communist country of Romania is there a thriving and growing Torchbearer Centre, but not far away in Albania, another was established in 2001. Mark Stoscher, the director, describes it as the result, not of a small happening, but rather a very big one this time—the war in Kosovo.

In 1999, in the midst of that war, thousands of Kosovar Albanians, about 600,000 of them, came to Albania. Mark says that their small church began caring for one thousand refugees. They received a gift of funds for a building to provide housing for refugees in the southeast of Albania at which time, Klaus came into partnership with the project. Most refugees returned to Kosovo when the war ended; but Mark, with cooperation from Schloss Klaus, began holding summer camps for people from all over Albania and Kosovo, followed by a six-month Bible school. Soon Torchbearers Albania was born. Throughout the summer now, about fifteen hundred campers are accommodated, and twenty-five students can attend the Bible school program in the winter months. God surely turned the tide in that formerly Communist country.

Torchbearers Switzerland

It was but a few years after Capernwray Hall was opened that Ian was invited to minister in churches and YMCA groups in Switzerland. Who would not take the opportunity to visit beautiful Switzerland? As a result, Swiss young people began to visit Capernwray in England and to attend the Bible School. Returning home, a number of these young people caught the fire of Torchbearing and organized visits to other Centres available at that time.

Elias Zürrer returned later to Capernwray Hall to find himself in the old dungeons. Over a period of time, our maintenance staff had been working away at installing electric lights, laying floors and cleaning up those "dungeons," while in one area, a large printing press was set up. Our Swiss friend, Elias, happened to be an expert printer—not a prisoner, although he may have felt like one, away down under the main building. It was not long, however, before he had produced our own Capernwray brochures, some tracts written by "Uncle Van" and some of Ian's first books.

Another young Swiss man, Christian Zehnder, sold some of those books, since he became manager of the Capernwray Bookshop for a time, not down in the dungeons, of course, but in the main building.

Ueli Zurrer, brother of Elias, had taken part in a "Mission Service Team" operating overseas at that time from Capernwray. Upon returning from one of these mission assignments in Nepal, Ueli and Ruth Zürrer now felt prompted to share Christ with their own people. This resulted, by God's enabling, in their finding an old but attractive home on which Ueli worked very hard to establish a small Torchbearer Centre in Switzerland. As Ruth described it, "Younger and older people filled our house as summer and winter activities were offered including a Bible School." That was in 1976. In the late 1990s, a reorientation took place due to changing circumstances so that, while the Zürrers continue to minister as faithful Torchbearers, we are now operating in a larger base near Interlaken in the famous Jungfrau region of Switzerland. The facility, with accommodation for up to 120 guests, has been made available for Torchbearer programs under the leadership of Daniel Blaser, formerly on staff at Klostermühle, Germany.

Germany: Bodenseehof

In the late 1950s, it "so happened" that Ian was invited to speak at Columbia Bible College in South Carolina, and that he "happened" to talk with an American student named Charlie Moore. Charlie mentioned that after college, he felt God was calling him to minister in Germany, though he did not have sufficient knowledge of the language. Ian had a great idea to help him. In recent months, as we traveled in Germany, there were, on occasions, welcome openings given to visit boys in boarding schools, which were common in Germany following the Second World War. At the invitation of the headmaster, he was given the opportunity to speak in some of the classes about Christianity.

So the "great idea" was that Ian would try to find such a school where an English teacher was needed, and Charlie Moore would apply.

When Charlie had graduated from Columbia Bible College, he spent two years teaching English in a German boarding school, at the same time learning German for himself from his students and others. Then Charlie felt led to open a youth center, which he named Bodenseehof, in the south of Germany, built with the support of a group of pastors and businessmen to accommodate one hundred people. Situated on the shore of Lake Constance and with Switzerland on the opposite side, Bodenseehof later became, and continues to be, an attractive Torchbearer Centre offering summer youth weeks and a winter Bible school.

Spain: Rio Vida

Switzerland may have its snowcapped mountains and exciting skiing, but what about Spain where it is claimed, at least in Alicante where the Torchbearers Centre is now situated, that they enjoy more than three hundred days of sunshine per year? The "happening" which God used to open the door for Torchbearers in Spain was part of the coming to Christ of Peter, the hitchhiker, in Germany. On Peter's return home to Hamburg, the first person with whom he shared his newfound joy was his good friend Reimar. Within a few weeks, Reimar wholeheartedly accepted Christ, and soon afterwards, attended the very first Bible school at Klostermühle. It was there that he met his Spanish wife, Ada. After further Bible training in Germany, Reimar and Ada were married in 1963; then they decided to go to Spain, hoping that one day there would be a Torchbearers Centre, perhaps in Ada's own home town of Valencia. They did indeed find a place, which they considered might be suitable for Torchbearers. The building, right on the beach of the Mediterranean Sea, was called "Mar Cristalino"—Crystal Sea. When Ian came to see it, he recognized God's handwriting in it as he had done in other similar situations. Following the making of some improvements—Reimar was originally a well-trained professional painter/decorator—and after furnishing the house, it was opened for "business" and, of course, people certainly came

Reimar and Ada spent almost thirty years Torchbearing. It was hard but satisfying work, with Ada doing almost all the good Spanish cooking. Ada is now at home with her Lord, whom she served so faithfully at Mar Cristalino and in ministry afterwards with Reimar in her own country.

Mar Cristalino was in a well-situated place, and God wonderfully impacted the lives, not only of Spanish folks, but of very many others who came and met with Christ in that attractive place. However, the time came when the local city government decided that Mar Cristalino was built right where it had planned to build a promenade for tourists and the local residents. They decided to demolish our building, and they promised to compensate Torchbearers, which they did. On hearing the news, Ian simply announced, "That's not the end of Torchbearing in Spain." Nor was it, because it "so happened" that there was a keenly evangelical pastor living just a two-hour drive from Mar Cristalino in Valencia who had heard Ian preach in Florida and had brought home a set of sermon tapes, to which the whole family listened regularly at devotions. As the children grew up, they used to wonder why, on occasions when they were free from school, they had to help their dad, Paco Platillero, make additions and alterations to their house, which he had already named "Rio Vida" (River of Life). Those children had not quite understood that their father had persistently cherished the hope that one day there would be enough rooms in their house to develop a small Bible school. On hearing that Mar Cristalino was now not to be "in action" any more, Paco contacted Ian to say that their home, Rio Vida, was available. After renovations, alterations and the building of a meeting room in 1998, the few helpers at Rio Vida, along with Paco and his wife and family, opened the doors of the home; and with great joy, they received a group of young people from England. Their visit and transport had all been arranged at Capernwray, and the group was led by long-term staff member Sue Gilmore, registrar for the Capernwray Bible School.

Now, being as enthusiastic as his dad, Paco, once was about the use of their home as a Bible school, and after attending the Capernwray School in England with his wife, Paul Platillero became the first director at Rio Vida, followed later by his brother Joe. Paul has said: "The family sermon tapes have now been replaced by the DVD series 'Rediscovering Christ' by Major Thomas so that the heart of the message remains the same—the centrality of Christ in the Christian." Both conference weeks and the winter Bible school terms are well attended, especially by those who enjoy sunshine and the nearby beach. Guests and students are fed with tasteful Spanish cooking and, much more importantly, with the life-giving and challenging Word of God.

Greece: Kingfisher Project

Another Torchbearer Centre in Europe is what we might call "definitely different." People may enjoy climbing mountains, skiing or sun bathing; but Theo Goutzios, who grew up in Australia of Greek parents, and his wife, Sandra, from England were active in the Lord's service in Greece, offering guests the chance to go sailing. Sailing, they thought, was an activity popular in that country so why not use it for God's glory as Theo was the skipper of a sailing ship? It so happened that this couple had been working as missionaries in Greece, largely involved with youth work, and in particular would organize open-air evangelistic meetings on the islands, taking young folk on board. It also happened that Theo and Sandra had attended the Bible school in Tauernhof, Austria ,in 1984, where Hans Peter Royer was the director, having replaced Gernot, who, to our deep sorrow, had died following an accident when testing out a paraglider in Austria.

Later on Theo, having resigned from his mission board in 1995, happened to meet up again with Hans Peter in Australia, sharing with him his desire to establish a Bible training program in Greece in association with Torchbearers. So there they are, responsible for and living on the sailing ship "Encounter," which was offered to them for a Torchbearer Centre "with a difference." Guests who come on board for summer retreats, in addition to the Bible school, sleep right on the ship. Students and visitors take their turns in manning the four sails and the spinnaker, also cleaning the decks, and sometimes sharing Bible truths in places, such as Philippi, where the apostle Paul preached. My sons delight to be invited to teach on the ship in Greece, and I am glad that their dad taught them how to handle the sails well on our family holidays. They enjoy sailing and, far more importantly, their father also taught them by example to handle God's Word to the blessing of themselves and their hearers. Theo, of course, always takes on board a crewman for the purpose of handling the sails, and the students undergo intensive sail training as part of the course. He says, "When storms strike, those most able lend a hand and keep the boat safe, but I am largely dependent on my crewman."

At the time of this writing, the time has come for Theo and Sandra to have their home, not just on "Encounter," but in a building on an island close to the mainland. Sandra has provided really good meals on board, but now, we trust, a building will be available before long where not only will the cooking be made more manageable, but there can be greater comfort for those who are attending the summer weeks and Bible school. There will still be great sailing days, but also some added comfort, since folks will not be on board all day and night. We anticipate that in the new building there will be a small dining and living area, and ultimately cabins for sleeping. When on the water, students may well remember from Scripture how the Lord Jesus spent time with his disciples on Galilee and how many lessons they learned. May students and guests learn some of God's important lessons on board our own "Encounter."

Sweden: Holsby

It was interesting, as Capernwray and the ministry of Torchbearers became increasingly known by people from various organizations and from churches of different denominations that among our guests increasing numbers of people were joining us from foreign countries. The word had traveled! At one time, a number were coming from Norway, and Ian considered that perhaps God had plans for Torchbearers in Scandinavia. He asked a young German man named Christian Bastke to travel to Norway, find somewhere to live, meet up with Norwegians and direct a spring Bible school program from 1971 to 1973.

Christian Bastke was, years before, just a typical German schoolboy whom Ian met when speaking on one occasion in Christian's school class. It became obvious then that though his name was Christian, he had no interest in becoming one. Ian saw an opportunity he could not resist, inviting the boy to visit Capernwray once he had finished high school. Christian did go to England and in his own words, he explained what happened: "A short time later the Major explained to Christian the message of salvation and introduced him to Jesus Christ. Accepting Jesus Christ as his personal Savior and Lord was a decision Christian never regretted and which proved to be life changing." After some time, he attended the Capernwray Bible School and also received further training in two other Bible colleges in the United States before beginning a teaching ministry himself.

Christian was ready and willing to accept Major's challenge. He found a suitable location on the coast of Southern Norway at the town of Kristiansand and began to minister among Norwegians. A couple from California, Fred and Sharon Wright, shared the work with Christian in the Bible schools before proceeding to Sweden. Meanwhile, many new contacts were made in Norway which still continues, through further visits by Christian and others. As an International Field Representative of the Torchbearers, Christian travels worldwide, serving the church as a true Torchbearer, even as he is also involved with other mission agencies.

In Sweden, Fred and Sharon Wright met a Swedish missionary to Japan, Mr. Karl Frandell, and his wife, who happened to have met Major Thomas at a missions conference in Japan. Knowing that Torchbearers worked with young people in holiday settings, Mr. Frandell suggested that Fred and Sharon should see a place named Holsby Brunn, which Mr. Frandell knew well since his mission group had held conferences in the buildings. Holsby Brunn was to be sold. The place was close to the area where Fred and Sharon were living and looking, on Major's behalf, for "a couple of acres" where a Torchbearer Centre could possibly be established. Realizing that probably God was not directing Torchbearers to Norway at this time, Major went to see Holsby Brunn and liked it very much. He contacted the Torchbearers board in the United States. Some good friends in Texas were willing to purchase the property and put it at the disposal of Torchbearers for use as a Centre until such time as repayment could be made. So it was that in 1973 the very first Torchbearer Bible School was established in Sweden about halfway between Stockholm and Copenhagen in an attractive and pleasant location where there is accommodation for up to 110 students in the Bible school or guests attending summer conferences.

The first director at Holsby Brunn—now known simply as Holsby—was obviously Fred Wright, followed by his good friend Wally Schoon and his wife, Donna. For a short time, it was a help to have a "real" Swede named Ulf Anderson as director, then Ric Schoon, son of Wally and Donna. Today I am happy that our grandson, Luke Thomas, was appointed recently as the principal of the Bible school. John Poysti, the current director, has the benefit of having a Swedish wife, who is able to help non-Swedes learn her difficult language. The staff at Holsby, seeking to encourage their neighbors in Sweden to know Christ, often do so by welcoming them to the Centre to join in the outdoor adventure facilities.

Holsby Brunn was formerly a quiet place—a health spa—where people could come and benefit by drinking the waters. Now Holsby Brunn—the word "Brunn" meaning a "spring in the area of Holsby"—is more often, after lectures and Bible teaching, a noisy place where students and guests may play games, climb ropes, walk in the surrounding forests and bring the local Swedish young people to do the same, seeking to introduce them to their friend, Jesus. Water from the spring is still flowing, although it is no longer used for drinking or health purposes. However, those who stay here or visit within Holsby Brunn, if they truly listen, may hear and, we pray, respond to Jesus when He says," If any man is thirsty, let him come to Me and drink." (John 7:37 AMP) He is, for anyone who comes and truly receives Him, the Water of Life, our Savior and Lord.

France: Champfleuri

"Parlez vous Francais?" If you do not speak French, then perhaps you should go to "Champfleuri." This place, situated about fifteen miles northeast of Grenoble, was started in 1955 under the leadership of two missionary couples, one French and the other American. These missionaries, who were working with The Bible Christian Union, bought the property, which I understand was a ruin at that time, but later they were able to run children's tent camps on the property. A group of Austrian Christians had been praying that a retreat center would be started in France for French youth. A family in Austria had come in contact with Peter Wiegand, through whom they came to know Christ, as did their small daughter, Gudrun, when visiting Schloss Klaus where the child went to a "Teenie Retreat." Gudrun grew up and attended a bilingual three-year Bible school near Paris, where she met and later married Blain, a young man from Texas. Blain and Gudrun spent three years working, studying and gaining experience in camping ministry at Schloss Klaus until they were assigned by Peter to the ministry of Champfleuri, meaning "flowery field." A few years later, the very first French-speaking, Torchbearer-affiliated Bible School opened, in 2005. The Bible school in France is named "DEFI" which, in French, means "The Challenge," and for students whose first language is not French, it could well be a challenge. It is, however, a good place to brush up on the language while studying God's Word. The desire of Torchbearers is that the ministry here in this part of France may develop and grow to become a blessing to many more people, young and old, who find their way to this spiritually needy part of God's world.

8

Crossing the Atlantic

I an and I never imagined, once having secured the "big house somewhere," that God would spread the influence of that Capernwray Hall and the title of "Torchbearers" around the world. The exact date of Ian's first invitation to travel and preach in the big world across the Atlantic is lost to history, but it was likely to have been in the early 1960s. At least I can remember the excitement of our sons when they were informed that Dad was to fly to America. In my childhood days, I was also told that my father traveled on business across the Atlantic, but then it had been on a big ship.

He sold hand-embroidered Irish linen from my grandfather's factory to wealthy Americans, until those "naughty" Texans and others introduced their much cheaper cotton. The process for weaving linen from our blue flax in Northern Ireland was much more complicated than growing cotton, but the linen it produced lasted more than twice as long. I rest my head at night on a pillow with a hand-embroidered linen cover more than one hundred years old. The factory closed, my dad's business was bankrupt and he was taken to heaven when I was just twelve years old. My mother and her four children moved across town from our big house and garden to a little one with a small patch of grass. It was, therefore, no problem for me to marry a poor evangelist. It is clear from Isaiah 55:8 "For my thoughts are not your thoughts, neither are your ways my ways, declares the Lord," and God has reminded me very many times of this since that famous auction for Capernwray: "Oh how great is thy goodness which Thou hast laid up for them that fear Thee; which thou hast wrought for them that trust in thee before the sons of men!" (Ps. 31:19, kjv). I continue to discover more of that goodness almost daily.

The "Mules"

Ian crossed the Atlantic many times since those early days, resulting in much blessing to many people and in the establishment of three active Torchbearer Centres in the United States, two in Canada, and one in Costa Rica. Some of the early invitations to Ian to preach in North America were possibly received as a result of his first book, *The Saving Life of Christ*, which was published in 1961 by Zondervan. Pat Zondervan, cofounder of the publishing house, along with his brother Bernie, became a very good friend and trusted advisor. Ian soon began to receive invitations from pastors of churches throughout the United States and Canada to teach for a full week in their churches. As well as evening meetings, in some instances, there would be both lunch hour meetings and occasionally "extras," such as businessmen's or school meetings. At first, the length of visiting and preaching in America might last a few weeks, then it extended eventually to three, or even four months, every year. On some occasions I could join Ian for a week or two during those times. I was always happy to meet with the women of churches where my husband preached and taught.

His messages were clear, and they lasted usually more than an hour—on occasions too much more for some people. The content fully, and from every part of God's Word, explained what Ian had, in tears at the age of nineteen, discovered for himself, that without Christ he was indeed a "hopeless failure." For seven weary years following his conversion he had been, as the Lord seemed to say, "hopelessly busy on my behalf," and for all his busyness, there were no results. Had not Jesus himself said, "the Son can do nothing of his own accord, but only what he sees the Father doing?" (John 5:19) So also in John 15:5, we hear Jesus say, "apart from me *you* can do nothing" (emphasis added). Then to his joy and relief, words Ian had read often but not acted upon came, as he testified many times. He heard: "to me to live is Christ," "when Christ, who is our Life appears," "I am crucified with Christ, nevertheless I live, for Christ lives *in* me," "reconciled by His death, we are saved by *His Life*" (paraphrased from Phil. 1:18; Col. 3:4; Gal. 2:20; Rom. 5:10). No wonder from that experience Ian's first book was entitled *The Saving Life of Christ* and his last was *The Indwelling Life of Christ.*

It was not until the Friday night of a week of meetings that with great enthusiasm Ian would show slides in those early days of some of the Centres which God had enabled Torchbearers to establish in various parts of the world. He rarely mentioned any need for financial support, nor that he had much part in the establishment of the Centres, since preaching the truth he had understood about an indwelling Lord and Savior captivated his heart and was his greatest passion. However, there were those friends who realized the need of support for such a wide-spreading ministry and took the opportunity to offer donations, for which we are still grateful. Soon Ian invited, and indeed *needed*, young men to travel with him, not only to carry the baggage, for which reason he jokingly would call them "mules," but because they meant so much more to him. They recorded the messages, managed a book table, answered questions, made travel plans and typed many letters, among other duties. There were always Ian's books available at the book table, as well as those from other writers with a similar message regarding the centrality of Christ in the believer. Ian's sermons were all recorded on tape by his "mule," so he had to be present at every single meeting. These tapes also were sold, and on occasions I still hear from friends who continue listening to the old recordings in their car as they travel on long journeys. Proceeds from the book table were frequently sent toward the support of Torchbearer staff, new ministries and building projects.

It was no easy assignment for the "mules" in all of this, since their travel day was normally Saturday, then another week of meetings would begin on the very next day. Most mules were young men who, because of their studies, had limited time to stay on the job, but they had opportunities to learn a lot. Frank Cirone, an American, was one who spent almost a year as Ian traveled to speak at conferences, conventions and in churches, as well as visiting the Torchbearer Centres to teach in the Bible schools. Frank became such a well-taught mule that he is currently the director and principal at our Torchbearer Centre at Ravencrest in Colorado. Mark Broughton, an Englishman who as a child was brought to Capernwray many times by his faithful parents, learned a lot as a mule for ten years—and survived. Almost two years ago, we organized a "mules weekend" here at Ravencrest—how they enjoyed sharing together.

United States, Colorado: Ravencrest Chalet

Ravencrest Chalet in Colorado is yet another Torchbearer Centre. Established in 1974, the chalet was truly the result of yet another "little happening." Ian had accepted an invitation to speak at a church in Colorado, but an offer had also been sent to Dr. Redpath from the same church for the same time, a mistake which turned out to be the "little happening" which God used to secure beautiful Ravencrest Chalet for Torchbearers. Ian gladly accepted an invitation to minister at another church in the area for the same week and was hosted by friends living in a nearby property with the name "Ravencrest Chalet." Designed as an exact replica of a Swiss chalet, Ravencrest functioned as a private home until Mr. Carl Vogel, a retired farmer who, along with his son and two other Christian businessmen, had purchased the property prior to the death of the owner and turned it into a bed-and-breakfast. However, the four businessmen had a vision for Ravencrest beyond that.

Desiring that the chalet be used for God's glory, they wondered if Major Thomas would be interested in using Ravencrest as a Centre for Torchbearers. Ian's reaction was initially negative. However, he thought and prayed long and hard about the question, until he felt God was saying "yes." It took many years, but being already furnished, Ravencrest was opened for business with Christian Bastke as director for a brief time, followed by our son Mark, then by Chris, who later appointed Wayne Weissman. Now, former mule Frank Cirone has the director's position!

In the summer months, Ravencrest Chalet rings to the sounds of teenagers in a typical youth program, while through snowy winters until spring, students at the Bible school discover the wonders of God's Word and enjoy all there is of the majestic

Rockies. As someone in the know has reported: "Ravencrest has been home to hundreds of Bible school students, a place of rest to numerous retreat guests and an opportunity for growth to countless teenagers. Above all, Ravencrest has been a vessel to display the glorious life of Christ Jesus our Lord!"

United States, Colorado: Timberline Lodge

Timberline Lodge, which is situated 8,500 feet above sea level, is a second Torchbearer Centre in Colorado, having been more recently added to the "family." "Happening" to attend Upward Bound and Bible School at Tauernhof, Austria, instead of remaining in the family business in Colorado, Brad Keirnes met his Canadian wife, Jane, in 1985 and served in Austria on staff from 1984 to 1986. On returning home to re-enter the family business, to which God was adding His blessings, it became possible for Brad to search for and acquire a place in the Rocky Mountains, so to fulfill their deepest shared desire to establish an alpine adventure ministry similar to Tauernhof.

In June of 1995, God directed them to "Timberline Lodge," situated near the Winter Park Resort and already operating commercially for skiing enthusiasts. It was available for purchase, so Brad took care of this and founded a board of directors and obtained staff, some of whom he had come to know at Tauernhof and who led those early operations, until Timberline was donated to Torchbearers in 2007. We are truly grateful for those hard-working staff members who have gone before in establishing such a very special place where young, and sometimes older, guests in outdoor programs, or students at Bible school, may enjoy God's amazing creation of snowy mountains, blue skies and the very best of skiing.

United States, Texas: His Hill

From mountain heights to peaceful lowlands, the third Torchbearer Centre in the United States is located in the great state of Texas. The inevitable "happening," however, was small this time. Situated an hour's drive from San Antonio in what the Texans call "the hill country," and near the small town with the pleasant name of Comfort, His Hill indeed stands on a hill with the Guadalupe River running below. That area was originally owned by a church in San Antonio, where the members were allowed to build vacation homes in order to leave behind their town homes during the hot summer weather. A church had been built on the hill with windows looking out on both sides to the view below. However, the church wished to sell the property, and it had been purchased by Johnnie Merchant, a business-woman and member of the San Antonio Church. This lady now had her own house built on the hill. However, her deepest desire was that the property would become a Christian camp for children and young people, though she hardly knew where to begin.

Of course, God knew because it so happened that Johnnie had a friend with whom she discussed her deepest desire. This friend happened to have a son studying at Columbia International University who knew that one of his fellow students was the son of a certain Major Ian Thomas, who was involved in that kind of business. Her friend knew where Major Thomas could be located in the United States, so it was possible for Johnnie to phone him and explain the situation. His almost immediate answer in so many words was, "Not interested!" However, he phoned back the following day to say, "I was not interested, but God is!" So on that day and with God's assurance, Ian made a long-term lease arrangement with Johnnie Merchant for the use of the property by Torchbearers. Her desire was truly fulfilled, in 1975 when the first Bible school took place, and in the summer of 1976 when kids at the very first camp were running all around her property.

The Bible school has about forty or fifty students yearly, studying in the old church, which is used as their lecture hall. Many students are Americans, but some come from Canada, Germany, and other countries as well. In the summer months, Johnnie, for many years before she was taken to heaven, saw her desire satisfied. The staff continues to serve around one thousand young campers every summer; campers who certainly have enjoyed the excellent facilities, including horse riding, swimming, climbing and archery. Most important of all, they sit around the campfire and hear about our Lord Jesus, who loves them and waits for them to love and to come to know Him. Hundreds have done so in the last thirty-five years.

Charlie McCall, the director at His Hill, is ably assisted by his wife, Patsy, and a faithful staff. He is a graduate of His Hill Bible School, Columbia International University, and Dallas Theological Seminary. He keeps standards high, as those before him did, and Christ at the very heart of the entire ministry.

Canada: Capernwray Harbour

Our creator God has planted Torchbearer Centres in many parts of the world, each one totally different in every way, even as their geographical situation differs, but all have come from His good hand through the response of thousands of people. No two countries could be more dissimilar than Canada and Costa Rica, but in both places, as elsewhere, the same God has provided a home where *He is at home* and is Himself the very reason for their existence. Big Canada, with its almost four million square miles of land and thirty-four million people, is surely in contrast to little Costa Rica, where you can cross coast-to-coast in three hours and where just about four-and-a-half million souls live.

Though Canada is a huge country, it also contains some small islands. In the Georgia Strait, just east of Vancouver Island, there are a number of them. The Torchbearer Centre is situated on Thetis Island. Charlie Fordham, son of evangelists to India, and who was born and educated there, emigrated to Canada and married his Canadian wife, Marlene, who agreed that God was calling them to full-time Christian ministry. Knowing they would require training in a Bible school, while visiting the home of friends, they happened to see a copy of a Christian magazine in which there was in the corner of one page a very small notice giving the address of the Bible school at Capernwray Hall, England. So it was that the Fordhams came to attend that very Bible school in 1971–72, which was at that time led by our long-time friend "Uncle Van."

Returning to Canada after Bible school, Charlie and Marlene spent four years in evangelistic ministry, during which time they saw many people come to a vital relationship with Jesus Christ. One day, Charlie and Marlene happened to meet a Canadian missionary, who explained that the mission to which he belonged had a building and ocean-front property, formerly used as a base camp for training of missionaries to indigenous people groups. The mission now wished to sell it. It was situated on Thetis Island in the Georgia Strait between the Vancouver coast and the east coast of Vancouver Island. When the Fordhams had opportunity, they drove to the little town of Chemainus and, with the car on a ferry, reached their destination in only twenty-five minutes. They found the building and property close to the beach and adjacent to the dock at which the ferry moored.

The property of about one hundred acres had much potential, even though the buildings and surrounding grounds were in serious need of practical development, refurbishment and restoration. Messages were sent to Major Thomas, who came to see the possibilities for Torchbearers. Having had the experience of viewing previous locations and knowing that a Torchbearer Centre required an attractive base for summer youth ministries, combined with suitability for Bible school programs, Major obviously took time to seek God's mind. There was no easy answer to what he knew would be the financial cost. However, suitable arrangements were finally made with the owners of the property, and it was not long before Charlie and Marlene had "moved house" with their two preschool children, Chris and Jessica. A team of young folk worked very hard with the Fordhams, who then named the first Canadian Torchbearer Centre most appropriately—"Capernwray Harbour Bible Centre." Having landed at Thetis Island on Friday, January 13, 1979, the team opened the very first Bible conference on a Friday three months later for the weekend of April 13, 1979, thus leading to the summer youth and adult retreats. winter Bible school followed in September, 1979, and ever since, for over thirty-three years, God has used this increasingly beautiful place to bring blessing, joy and fun to thousands of folks from many countries.

Under the faithful leadership of Charlie and Marlene Fordham, the staff continues to welcome all who come to share in a week, or a whole year, of fellowship, with Christ-centered teaching in this "building and gardens by the sea." Canadians love the place, as do Germans and very many others, and with many excellent amenities, it is never dull at Capernwray Harbour Bible Centre.

Canada: Capernwray Quebec

As an outreach of Capernwray Harbour, French Quebec also has its own Torchbearer Centre, which humanly speaking, came into being through the work of a married couple who had attended the Bible school at Capernwray Harbour. Paul Mathon was born and educated in the Canadian province of Quebec, the largest in the whole of Canada. Paul's wife, Judy, was from British Columbia, where they first met. After studying God's Word at Capernwray Harbour, they knew clearly that God was calling them to bring the proclamation of the life of Christ in the teaching of God's written Word to Quebec. Returning there, and under the direction of the board of Torchbearers at Capernwray Canada, the Mathons began their ministry. Not having the money needed to purchase property, Paul and Judy moved to a couple of different locations for a few years, and local people began to take an interest in the ministry of God's Word. Finally, they were led to yet another property, which had once been a camp and was set in 120 acres in an area just over an hour from Montreal in the heartland of tourist areas of Quebec. The woodland is a natural habitat for Canadian beaver and many species of birds and animals. Established in 1993, this Torchbearer Centre in Quebec, as an offshoot from the Centre miles away on Thetis Island, British Columbia, is suitably named "Capernwray Quebec." With accommodation for sixty-five people, the Centre boasts a small swimming pool and other amenities. The one-year, short-term English Bible school programs take place from September to May, with conferences throughout the summer months. Most people who live in Quebec speak French and for students in our Bible school, it has not been easy to make contact with the neighbors, however I was truly delighted to discover that at a recent "open day," at least one hundred "locals" came to visit.

We trust that God will increase such opportunities to introduce many more folks in Quebec to Christ. I am so glad that He once found a boarding-school kid in India and overruled his plans so that one day, as a faithful Torchbearer, he might be used to share the joy of his Lord in the big country of Canada.

Costa Rica: Portantorchas

It was one of God's simple happenings which opened the way in Costa Rica for the development of a permanent Torchbearer base in that country. In 1968, Ian had been invited to speak at a Spanish language institute for missionaries in the capital, San Jose, where Marco Perez, a medical student in the local university, was teaching Spanish part-time. For that reason, they came to know each other, and Ian invited Marco to attend the Bible school at Capernwray Hall. Marco was blessed, not only by studying God's Word, but also by meeting his wife, Janet, who came from California. After they married, Ian visited the couple, and together they often discussed the possibility and the need for establishing a Torchbearer Centre and Bible school in Costa Rica. Finally, in 1991 Marco asked, "When are we going to start?" According to Marco, Ian said, "Today . . . let's find a place." Marco and Janet had already located an attractive and suitable large property just six miles from San Jose, which had been taken by a bank foreclosure. A very friendly manager offered excellent terms—20 percent of the appraised value, no down payment, no mortgage, and the bank would assume taxes for two years, with four years to pay without interest. "This is how we bought Portantorchas," Marco says. In 1992, although work was being done on the property, summer camps for children were held, and by August of 1993, the first Bible school started with just one student. Much labor has made "Portantorchas" a very lovely place, set in an attractive garden area with a pond, able to accommodate approximately thirty-six people. It is located in a town called Coronado, just six miles north of the capital city, yet fairly secluded.

Lectures at the Bible school are given in Spanish and English, with simultaneous translation available. Students may also come early and receive some teaching in Spanish. Apart from the Bible school program, Portantorchas staff continue to work well with local children, keeping a busy schedule throughout the year. They also host mission teams, local conferences and ministry training. Staff takes advantage of the days without guests or students to improve the grounds and buildings. People of many nationalities have attended the Bible school at Portantorchas, not simply to learn about the Bible, but to be blessed by coming to know more personally that life-changing One, our Lord Jesus, about whom that Bible speaks.

Although the majority of students are from Canada, the United States and Costa Rica, it is amazing how people from so many other countries have found their way to this place. The following have all been represented in the last eight years: Peru, Cuba, Honduras, Venezuela, Argentina, Ecuador, Bolivia, Switzerland, Germany, Austria, Belgium, Bolivia, Panama, Norway, Denmark, Australia and Mexico. That sounds like the "United Nations"—but united in "Someone!"

9

Torchbearers Venturing East

Malaysia: Harvest Haven

In 1973, when Ian Thomas visited Singapore at the invitation of the Singapore Keswick Convention Committee to speak, he never realized that he would meet up with the future director of a Torchbearer Centre in Malaysia. He had anticipated meeting with a young man named John Lee, but searching in a telephone book for the young man's name, Ian found several pages of men called John Lee, that being as common a name as John Smith in England. Abandoning the search for this name in a telephone book, it so happened that another John Lee came after one particular meeting to have a talk. This John Lee, just nineteen years of age, explained that he was expecting to study civil engineering in Glasgow, Scotland in 1974 and hoped to find a really evangelical church in the city. Following their conversation, Ian asked the young man to keep in touch with him and prayed with him before they parted. John has said, "I felt like God was about to do something in my life."

In September 1974, John began his studies at the University of Strathclyde and spent the following Christmas at Capernwray Hall. Then, after graduation in 1976 and knowing that God had probably more for him in life than being an engineer, John asked about attending the Bible school at Capernwray. This he did before returning to Malaysia in 1977. While in Bible school, God laid on his heart a dream and vision to establish a Torchbearer Centre in Malaysia. Meanwhile, and unknown to him, a young lady, Joyce, who was also from Malaysia, came to study in Manchester, England, and was led to Christ through her housemate, another Malaysian, Marie Lo, three months before her graduation. She was encouraged to attend the Capernwray Bible School to prepare for her return home to an idolatrous environment in Malaysia. Joyce attended Capernwray Bible School for three months, until December 1981, and while she was there, Joyce heard about John Lee during her workday duties with Mrs. Alan Redpath. When she returned to Malaysia, she visited John. She was quick to share John Lee's dream of establishing a Torchbearer Centre in Malaysia. After three years, they were married in their hometown of Penang. John was working in a consulting engineers' office, while at the same time our happy couple was all over town teaching Bible studies, ministering in churches, and to groups in their own home. On occasions the apartment of a friend was used for "mini" Torchbearer weekends; John also used to arrange meetings for Ian to introduce the young and old to understand the reality of our true Christian life in Christ.

On five occasions, John took leave from work to travel with the major in America, assisting him three months at a time, and happy to be his "mule" for short periods. There were by then, two children in the Lee family, and John felt again a strong calling to minister Christ in his own country by developing a Torchbearer residential Centre. To prepare more fully, the whole family moved to South Carolina in 1993 so that John and Joyce could attend Columbia Bible College and Seminary for three years, while the children attended a Christian school there. That was a very helpful experience after which John Lee—who, after all, was not the John Lee whom Ian had intended to meet—was more convinced than ever that an all-knowing God would open the way for a Torchbearer Centre in Malaysia. So many of his own countrymen had never even heard of God's only Son, Jesus Christ, Savior of the world.

In God's good time, a piece of land was donated for the ministry in a small town called Gopeng, near the city of Ipoh at the foothills of the well-known Cameron Highlands. The town is about two hours' drive north from the capital city of Kuala Lumpur and a few hundred kilometers from Singapore, where this story first began. Friends of Torchbearers from many places, including Malaysia, supported the new project. A kind friend in America, in her gratitude for the ministry of Torchbearers in her life, gave a large gift so that it was not long before beautiful "Harvest Haven" was built and functional with a small Bible school, holiday conferences, and Bible camps in place.

Indonesia: Pondok Kepenrey

When we first settled at Capernwray Hall away back in 1946, during the coldest winter in living memory, we made our home in what for the Marton family had been the "nursery wing" of the house. It consisted of three good-sized bedrooms, all with fireplaces, and there was even a tiny bathroom. However, Ian reckoned that our family would be using space which could easily allow for dormitories for about fourteen of our expected guests, none of whom should be turned away for lack of space. So it was that later we moved our home to a nearby corridor with three much smaller rooms overlooking the courtyard. One slightly larger room was, some years later, made into two rooms, one being extra small for two young sons. Our corridor then gave access to guests or students from our side of the house leading to the main staircase and the ground floor. In our sons' little room, there was just about space to squeeze between the beds. However, those small boys were delighted when guests or students walked along our corridor, and they made sure their door was kept wide open as long as possible, so that those kind "friends" would drop by and give them sweets or read the bedtime story. One day I found the door closed but with a sign on the outside in childish writing: "Knock and it shall be opened unto you, come in and it will be closed after you." I was pleased they actually knew the Scripture, at least their own translation, but I was somewhat embarrassed at their impudence.

However, when I had time to observe the view to the courtyard from our adjacent room in that corridor, I found it an interesting and busy place. One winter morning during Bible school, I noticed a particular student whose duty it was every morning before classes to clean out the old dustbins, usually overflowing with all kinds of dirty trash, in a small covered corner alongside some steps. With a well-worn brush and shovel, the young man had to sweep out that filthy place and take the rubbish in a wheelbarrow outside the courtyard area to another location, usually making more than one journey to complete the job. From my window, I observed a most diligent and reliable young man doing the work of a servant regularly and very thoroughly, day after day. On closer inspection, about which he had no idea, I noticed that every last speck of rubbish was carefully brushed up and removed, leaving the place amazingly clean and tidy until the next day. I thought, "That young man will one day become a good leader." He was Jimmy Kawilarang from Indonesia.

In the 1970s, Ian had met an Indonesian evangelist in Germany, who introduced him to a fellow Indonesian Bible teacher and other pastors. Ian invited the Bible teacher to study at Capernwray, and he then introduced Torchbearers and the Bible school to Jimmy Kawilarang. Jimmy remained in England for further study elsewhere, while his fiancée Mandy, also from Indonesia, attended the Capernwray Bible School. Our son Mark married the two in an Indonesian church in London. But no, that is not the end of the story.

On their return home, Jimmy was appointed pastor of a church in Jakarta, and in 1983 he started Torchbearers by holding a "Mini Bible School" in Java following which, on August 1, 1984, Jimmy was appointed as national director by Major Thomas. This, of course, was not for the country of Indonesia, but for Torchbearers. It was some time before a piece of land was found in West Java, near the small town of Cipanas, sixty miles from the capital of Jakarta. With financial support from many friends of Torchbearers, as well as hard work, Jimmy toiled, as he had done on his Bible school assignment years before. Now, along with his local laborers, he worked until "Pondok Kepenrey" (Capernwray Lodge) with its fine gardens and accommodation for 120 folks was opened on April 21, 1985.

Jimmy and Mandy have continued to maintain this ministry, as true and faithful Torchbearers, often through difficult times and circumstances, for almost twenty-seven years. Jimmy has much about which to be happy, just as he writes: "Praise the Lord that since Major first came to Indonesia until now many

Indonesians have come to faith in Jesus at Pondok Kepenrey and elsewhere as Major Thomas, his sons, myself and other Torchbearer representatives have shared the gospel of Christ in Indonesia."

Torchbearers Philippines

When Torchbearers ministry extended into Germany from Capernwray Hall in 1958 at "Klostermühle," we little imagined that in 1987, almost thirty years later, it would be reported from the Philippines, "The first student center for high school students was opened in 1987 in Quezon City." This came about through a former Torchbearer representative, the Rev. Bill Hekman, and continued by the Rev. David Hobson, son of Bob Hobson, who has taught in Torchbearer Bible Schools for many years. Techie Vargas attended that first student center and later, she and her husband, Loy, attended Capernwray Bible School in England. On their return to the Philippines, Loy was given the position of Philippines national director.

His passion for youth has led Loy to visit high schools, along with the staff he has trained, to present what are called Christian "value classes." Torchbearers was given permission to teach these classes in any school in the Philippines, with parents and teachers also present. Obviously, in a Catholic country the teaching of Christian living is acceptable, and Torchbearers explain the way very clearly. Young people also enjoy summer camps, which, along with the school teaching, have been arranged faithfully under the direction of our good friend and Torchbearer director Loy Vargas. However, we were greatly saddened very recently, even as this book was being written, to hear that our much loved and truly appreciated friend had not recovered from an illness, and God had taken him home to Himself. We understand that

Techie, who has been such a part of Torchbearing in the Philippines, will continue the ministry that Loy enjoyed for many years.

Those former students who at some time attended the Bible school at Capernwray Hall, may be interested to know that at one time Loy himself acknowledged, "Most of the principles in dealing with the students and doing outreaches were learned when at Capernwray Hall and the ten-day outreach at Bramhall." He also remembered Ian's advice: "You have the message to share with the students who visit the Centre. If you neglect the message you only become a recreational Centre." That was good advice, and under Loy's directorship, Christ was always at the heart of Torchbearers Philippines.

Japan: Yamanakako

We discovered early on that when young people come to stay at the youth center, they expect to find what we used to call in England a "tuck shop"—better known now as a snack bar. Finding a suitable small room was almost impossible in the early days at Capernwray, but one day I was observing an unused and partly open space under the large staircase which led to the bedrooms. There was even an old unwanted oak table from the Marton's time just fitting the space. So we managed to buy chocolates and other desired goodies from a wholesale warehouse, laid them out attractively on the table and opened for business twice daily. As Capernwray was four miles from the nearest town of Carnforth, and in those early days young people didn't possess cars, our little tuck shop became incredibly popular for many young, sugar-hungry guests. One evening, however, I happened to be on duty at the snack bar when my customers who, coming from the evening meeting, all arrived at the same time and pushed together hard against the Marton's table so as to be first in line. They pushed me too, until my back was held firmly between the table and the wall behind me, indeed pressed so hard that I could neither serve anyone nor get myself free, until a staff member came to the rescue. The net result was that I made a desperate appeal to my husband that very night to build a proper snack bar, if possible tomorrow!

Some months later, out in the old courtyard, the horses having long since died or been sold, I sat on a bench outside one of the stables which had been totally transformed, a sign overhead saying "Beehive." On the inside, tables and chairs were in place; and there was an impressive variety of sweet delights for sale on the counter, with coffee, tea and even milk shakes available.

Sitting on the courtyard bench drinking my cup of tea that afternoon, with no one else around, happy as I was to enjoy our new Beehive, I was much more interested in the figure of a somewhat small young man entering the courtyard under the high archway, slightly bent by his large and heavy backpack. Even more fascinating was the fact that he appeared to have come from Asia; until then, most of our foreign guests and students were European. I invited the stranger to come alongside me on the bench, soon discovering that he was Japanese. He had heard about Capernwray from a young Austrian man who had been sitting across the table at breakfast in the same youth hostel in London where he happened to be staying overnight. He said in his broken but understandable English, "That boy kept a big black book alongside his breakfast plate, as if someone might just steal it, so I enquired what it was all about. Rather shyly, he told me it was a Bible and was about God. I said I wanted to visit the place where he bought the book, so he suggested that I come here to this place and he gave me the directions."

I happened to know that the somewhat shy young man from Austria was Walter Thaler, on his way home from a visit to Capernwray, where I believe he came to know Christ and had probably bought the Bible at our bookshop. I knew also that Walter had an older brother named Ernst who, it so happened, became a true believer in the home of Peter our hitchhiker of some years earlier, when he and his wife, Runhild, first settled in Schladming, Austria.

The name of our new Japanese friend was Hideki Tanazawa, which he allowed us to shorten to "Tana." Having received a meal, Tana asked permission to look around Capernwray. He noticed our New Zealand "just-a-plumber," Haldane, working with his willing team building the new conference hall on the grounds and suggested that perhaps he could join them and stay to help. This was soon arranged. Tana was kindly welcomed to join the international team of young volunteers and heard them pray every morning before work to a God he did not even know.

This began to make an impression on him, although, as he said later, he never intended to become a Christian. However, as he explained to me on another occasion, "By meeting with Peter, your son, and working together on the team, my desire to become a Christian grew strong." This desire led to Tana's attending Capernwray Bible School, during which time he said, "I happily trusted in the Lord." Indeed what a joy! It is true, "The seeking soul shall find." Following this time, my husband arranged for Tana to study for two more years at a Scottish Bible school before returning to Japan, visiting German Torchbearers on the way. Happy to be home, Tana served at a church pastored by a German known to Torchbearers. On the pastor's return to Germany, Tana became the pastor of that church for another five years.

As was to be expected, Tana longed to establish a "Capernwray" in Japan, but how and where? In the meantime, he married a wonderful wife who has supported him fully in everything God enabled him to undertake in the following years. When Sachiko married Tana, she well knew that his heartfelt desire was to build and direct a Torchbearer youth center in Japan, where hundreds of Japanese like himself could find God and come to know Him in Jesus. Sachiko had already studied to be a dietician and this has, of course, aided her in how and what she cooks so that our Centre in Japan became well known for its excellent Japanese cuisine.

After a long search, a small section of land was found, south of Tokyo near Lake Yamanaka, with a clear view of the famous Mount Fuji. Ian had already visited Japan when Tana had arranged meetings for him, so when the available land was found, Ian was soon back there to give his approval, and plans were prepared. Tana had admired the windows at Klostermühle, Germany when he had visited there, so the German director kindly supplied the same type of windows as a gift to Torchbearers Yamanakako.

The grand opening took place in May 1987. In the course of time, Tana and Sachiko had four children, who had to learn to share their home with all the children, families and young people, as well as those from reunions and church groups who came to stay, while Sachiko cooked and Tana preached. Some years later, a next-door building became available. On one occasion when Ian was preaching at the Centre, with Tana interpreting, I walked around that empty building and prayed that it might become part of Torchbearers, which it did. This extra accommodation has been a great help. Though Tana and his wife will soon retire, he will continue to minister Christ in Japanese churches where he is well known. We are so grateful to God for the many Japanese who have met with a life-changing Savior at Japan Yamanakako because a young Austrian was not too shy to bring his Bible to breakfast. We also praise God for supplying Canadians Steve and Jen Frentz with courage to continue the leadership of Torchbearing at Japan Yamanakako.

India: Himalayan Torchbearers

"I, being in the way, the LORD led me" (Gen. 24:27, KJV). So said Abraham's servant after he had been sent to find, and did indeed meet, the right wife for his master's son, Isaac. I had no idea that I too, though unconscious of the outcome at the time, was "being in the way the Lord led me" when I chose India as my stopover place offered by the airline on a journey home to England. I had been with Ian for meetings in Australia but returned earlier than he after receiving a call from Elizabeth Alfred, a former Capernwray student living in Malaysia. Elizabeth had been asked to assist an Indian pastor, who was to direct a short-term Torchbearer Bible program in a school operated in a Swedish mission in India during their summer break. However, the pastor had broken his leg and was now unable to keep his commitment. On hearing that I happened to be in India at this time, Elizabeth asked if I could help, which I was happy to do. Need I say that the happenings which resulted in the later establishment of a most amazing Torchbearer Centre in India were two-fold: one was an airline's schedule, and the other was a pastor's broken leg.

It was in the town of Dehradun in the north west of India, where Elizabeth was already leading the small Bible school, that I met a fine young Indian named Satish John. In 1995 he had founded what is now known as "Himalayan Torchbearers" because it is obviously in sight of the great Himalayan Mountains.

Satish, having become a true believer in Christ, suffered greatly for that decision, not only physically, but also he was not allowed to return home ever again. During our days at the "mini" Bible school, where about twenty young and some older people joined us, a number of young men were our interpreters. Satish was the best of all. Not only was his spoken English excellent, but his love for and joy in Christ were obvious. Although it could be seen that Satish came from a high caste family, it amazed me that he was constantly busy sweeping floors, scrubbing tables, shopping for food in the "not so clean" local village and much more. What impressed me most was that whatever he did and wherever he had to go, Satish always wore a snow-white shirt.

God later made it possible for Satish to study at our Torchbearer Bible School in Australia, where he met Ian for the first time. He appointed Satish as field representative for Torchbearers India. This led later to the establishment of Himalayan Torchbearers in a very wonderful building—which is a story in itself—and is located in the foothills of the Himalayas, 240 kilometers north of Delhi. In 1988 Satish was married to Rajni, a woman we could well call a perfect fit for him. Their daughter, Zara, is currently studying at college in the United States. The Centre can accommodate 110 people, and the ministry consists not only of a six-month Bible school, which operates in the Hindi language, and a two-year leadership course, but also provides conference facilities for other Christian organizations. In 2013, they began a three-month Bible school from February to April. Over time, Satish and his staff have opened no less than seven elementary schools for underprivileged children in North India, with appointed Christian teachers, and one vocational training center for the physically handicapped. We do not know what is yet to follow in the ministry of Torchbearers in the country of India with its massive population of 1.2 billion. Torchbearers will be ready for God's directions, and it is our prayer that at Himalayan Torchbearers, very many more Indians will find a Christ who loves them, died for them and rose again to give them eternal life.

10

Torchbearers "Down Under"

Australia: Wongabri

When that first group of ten young British guests arrived at Capernwray Hall on May 3, 1947, to attend the very first week at our holiday center for young Christians, my husband Ian and I—not so very much older than our guests—little expected that over the many years we were to live there, the world was to come to us. Europeans, Americans, Canadians, Japanese, Indians, Malaysians, Indonesians, even numbers of folks from "down under" in Australia and New Zealand. Those and others have walked our corridors, enjoyed our gardens, sung our hymns and, most of all, have heard God speak. As a small child growing up, I often heard my mother and grandmother talk about a country called Australia, and my mother hoped one day to visit relatives in that huge land.

In the mid-1800s, two of my grandmother's brothers had sailed from Liverpool, England, to emigrate to Australia. One of the two was lost at sea, but the other arrived safely and later married. There were a number of relatives whom Mother always hoped to visit, and one cousin in particular with whom she corresponded throughout her life. Ian was invited to preach at Bible conferences and churches in many parts of the world, and I was able to accompany him on one particular occasion to Australia, where the opportunity came to meet some of those relatives on my mother's behalf.

It was in the early 1970s that Ian was staying in Sydney, Australia, while speaking at meetings in that area. He was kindly accommodated by some friends who were involved in missionary work. The wife spoke to Ian many times—at every single meal and sometimes between meals—about a very lovely home with extensive grazing land, whose current owner was a good Christian friend interested in selling the property. Ian's hostess thought he should consider the place for a Torchbearer Centre. This place was just about one-and-a-half hour's distance from Sydney, so Ian should indeed at least see it, she insisted. Even when Ian explained that he really had no thought of considering a Torchbearer Centre in Australia, the lady still persisted. He finally capitulated, and the couple was happy to drive him there. Ian did indeed like the place and could see its possibilities, both for a conference ministry as well as a Bible school, but was somewhat relieved to find that a buyer was expected to sign for the property the following day. However, during the night the owner felt God telling her to sell at a lower price, but only to Torchbearers. The prospective buyer was turned away. Ian considered that God's hand was indeed in the project and after much thought and prayer, he made the decision.

The happenings which were God's way of leading to a Torchbearer Centre in Australia would seem to have been brought about through one very persistent lady and another most obedient one. The house was simply a large and beautiful family home. There were wonderful gardens professionally designed and planted and all surrounded by about seventy acres of grazing for cattle. Extensive work has been achieved by staff, students, and volunteers over many years to provide the facilities required for conferences and Bible school, and that work still continues. A small river flows close to the property, which is named "Wongabri" (meaning, in the aboriginal language, "Bend in the River") and is part of a nature reserve. Students always knew they were in Australia when they could view the kangaroo on the far side, though recently the area has become a bird sanctuary.

Despite many hindrances in acquiring such a beautiful private property and converting it into a Torchbearer Centre, Ian worked along with good friends to make arrangements for the few hard working staff, including the director and his wife. Wongabri was opened as the first Torchbearer Centre in Australia near the town of Moss Vale, New South Wales, in the year 1972. Arranged mostly in small dormitories built on the grounds, it can accommodate about sixty people for conferences or Bible schools.

Our friend Haldane Rowan, wonderfully supported by his wife Thelma, is the current director. Mentioned earlier as "just a plumber," since that time he has served as a pastor and gained further experience of various ministries.

Local friends visit often, attending meetings and being involved in the outreach from Bible school. They host students in their homes, many of whom work with youth groups in the nearby churches and elsewhere. There is also a thriving ministry in Queensland with many Bible conventions being held throughout the state featuring Torchbearer speakers from around the world. This was primarily initiated by our good friend Richard Drew, who was himself greatly impacted by Ian's book *The Saving Life of Christ*.

Australia is the sixth largest country in the world, yet the population is a mere 22 million as compared with North America's population (including Canada) of about 347 million. Australians truly need to hear God's Word as proclaimed and lived out from this attractive and welcoming Torchbearer Centre. We are glad that even though the journey from other parts of the world is long and expensive, many students from other countries still find their way to Wongabri and leave with happy memories of the place and a deeper understanding of the life which is theirs in Christ. We trust and pray that more Australians will take advantage of the ministry available here in their own very big country. I understand that the Duke of Gloucester, when he was governor of Australia many years ago, enjoyed visits to Wongabri, and that Billy Graham stayed one night in the guest room during the 1969 crusade in Sydney. Fame for Torchbearers!

New Zealand: Monavale, Capernwray Crossing and Adventure Bible School

I had heard my husband say many times that as a small boy his main ambition in life was to keep sheep in New Zealand. Obviously this was not to be, but in fact he did make many visits to that beautiful country to feed God's Word to His "sheep people." As Psalm 100:3 states, "We are his people, and the sheep of his pasture," and the Lord Jesus in John 21:15 instructed Peter, "Feed my lambs." Again in verse 16, He told his disciple Peter, "Tend my sheep." So Ian made visits to New Zealand over a number of years sharing Christ and His Word in churches and at conferences and conventions in many cities and towns in both the North and South Islands.

He came to love the country and its people. Then it so happened that a young doctor, Tony Hanne, attended the spring Bible school at Capernwray with his wife June. They were planning to move to New Zealand to work in a medical practice in that country and discussed with Ian the possibility of establishing a Torchbearer Centre in New Zealand. God obviously had that in His mind. Were you to visit that country today, you could stay for a conference or for Bible school near the delightful town of Cambridge at a place called Monavale Homestead. This is not the original Torchbearer Centre, since we have moved twice from the first location, which was in Howick, Auckland. Our third son, Peter, like Peter in John 21, was asked by his human father to go to New Zealand and to "feed the sheep." Peter at first was needed to direct the Centre in Australia, where he met his wife, Elizabeth, following which he was sent to develop the ministry in New Zealand. Originally a farm with a fine large home on the property, Monavale Homestead was later used as a somewhat exclusive bed-and-breakfast and a function venue, but has now become a thriving Torchbearer Centre. Over the years we have added extensively to the original buildings so that Monavale Homestead accommodates over sixty students and guests. Like Wongabri in Australia, there are very lovely gardens surrounding the house, and there is a tennis court and small swimming pool on site. The work at Monavale never ends—just ask my son Peter.

Besides Monavale, there are two additional Centres as part of Torchbearers New Zealand. The first is The Capernwray Crossing in the town of Geraldine on New Zealand's South Island, where we offer a thirty-week Bible school, which operates under the leadership of Canadian Dale Epp and his wife, Patti. Students minister to young people and others in local churches. The second is The Adventure Lodge at Lake Karapiro is about thirty minutes from Monavale where Peter Bichan leads students in a six-week ABS—Adventure Bible School. Along with Bible teaching, Peter gives students an opportunity for real physical adventures in the lake, on the rivers and by hiking. Obviously you need to be physically fit for that one.

About the same time that Wongabri was established in Australia, the Torchbearer ministry also developed in New Zealand, a small, comfortable country where those who live there enjoy life with the many delightful beaches around the country, and the availability of all kinds of sports. Torchbearers from Monavale are concerned to use extensive community outreach, especially to young unchurched people around the country, as well as to older folks, with clear Christ-centered biblical teaching. There are conferences, functions and events held at the Centre to which local people can come throughout the year. My old "Major" was always delighted to know that the "sheep" he had once fed were continuing to receive God's good food from the next generation.

11

The Last Chapter–
But Not the End of the Story

If, as many people do before deciding to read a book, you have turned to this last chapter to see what mine is all about, then please go back to the beginning. This book is all about many seemingly unimportant "happenings" and life situations, which led to its writing—but they are the story.

My husband encouraged the growth of all the Torchbearer Centres over the years and built close relationships with many of those involved in the growing ministry. Ian had encouraged John Lee from Singapore in every way from the time he had first met him, so that even though Ian was nearing the age of ninety-two when the dedication of Harvest Haven in Malaysia took place in 2007, he insisted on being there. Chris asked his dad if he really thought he should make the long journey, and Ian's response was, "I will tell you when I get back." I then asked if he would please travel first class, and the response was a very definite, "No," but he finally, somewhat unwilling, consented to book business class. Mark, the faithful mule, accompanied Ian, and Chris met them in Malaysia. The dedication took place on May 27, 2007, with much thanksgiving to God for His goodness and faithfulness and celebrating a dream that became a reality after thirty years of waiting. John Lee suggested that Ian give, if he felt able, a brief message of about ten minutes, but it was reported to me that he spoke to those attending the dedication for at least an hour. When Ian returned home, somewhat the worse for wear, I was so grateful that our first-class Doctor Fonken, himself a missionary, came to us to take care of Ian, especially to treat his weary feet until he regained some strength. However, two months later on August 1, after only two nights in hospital, Ian died of pneumonia, along with other complications. Some of our family sang him to heaven with some of the choruses and hymns he had often led with such delight and enthusiasm at many meetings. When the night nurse came on duty before Ian left us, recognizing that we were British, she told us that her son was leaving home soon to attend a Bible school in England. I inquired if the name was Capernwray. It was! The Lord Himself seemed to have arranged just another little "happening" to remind us of His goodness, which still awaited us as He had promised so long ago (see Ps. 31:19).

Newly Born

I visited a newborn baby recently—just five and a half pounds in weight—like a tiny doll. His skinny, but long, arms and tiny, but long, fingers reached up and out of the baby blanket as if to greet me. Everything—absolutely everything—God created and set in just the right place for that tiny body, so that with its myriad cells, it would become a man. So it is when we, as newly born-again believers, real Christians are true to the function for which we were recreated in Christ. We have actually received in Him all that we need for God to use us as His children and for His purposes. The apostle Peter in his second book writes to believers, "His divine power has granted to us all things that pertain to life and godliness" (2 Pet. 1:3). That being so, it is to be our privilege to live in a relationship of love for, dependence on and obedience to Him, so that we are available to fulfill His plans and purposes for us—whatever those may be and whether we like them or not!

The "family" of Torchbearers, like the church, has come into being as a body of believers—no two Torchbearer members are alike, but all should be functioning, as far as they understand, as God intended and should be available to Him in very different ways. When the "Torchbearers of the Capernwray Missionary Fellowship" (our original and official title in the 1950s as decided by my husband, with prayer and with reliance on God) began, anyone who truly wished to become a member received a card signed by "W. Ian Thomas, Leader." You were assigned a number (ours of course were one and two), and the date you joined officially was noted. The address was simply "Capernwray Hall, Nr. Carnforth, N. Lancs" (no zip code etc. in those days), and the telephone number was merely "Carnforth 185." Simple and easy to remember.

However, the words inside the small folder with its Torchbearer emblem on the outside were not so simple, nor so easy, such as "Torchbearers are available to Christ 24 hours a day with all they are and have," and "Torchbearers accept the privilege of sacrificial giving, because all they possess is Christ's." There are nine separate statements on the inner first page, the ninth one being, "Torchbearers practice the daily reading of the Bible," and

First Thessalonians 5:18 states, "give thanks in all circumstances; for this is the will of God in Christ Jesus for you."

On the second page were ten items constituting the "Declaration of Faith," all of which make for the consideration of those who called ourselves "Torchbearers." Number eight declares, "I believe that a soul without Christ is lost, and that I have a solemn responsibility towards all men everywhere to warn them, and to win them, as the Holy Spirit at whose disposal I am, may lead them."

Finally, on the last page of the membership card were four more items headed "Member's Covenant," and as I now read the fourth item, I give thanks to God that those who today call themselves Torchbearers, especially if they live and work at Torchbearer Centres—from directors and Bible school principals with their wives and families, to every staff member—can honestly declare item number four: "I affirm my love for all real Christians everywhere, of whatever nation, class, creed or color, and associate myself with their needs, their labors and their sufferings." I always tell people who ask me about visiting any one of our Torchbearer Centres, wherever they may be found, "Yes, of course you may visit, and the staff there will be really delighted to welcome you." Often I add, just in case there should be the slightest doubt, "Tell the folk that 'Mrs. T' [which means Joan Thomas] sent you!"

It is also fascinating for us, though not for God, since He knows the end from the beginning, that Torchbearers really began with a boy of thirteen in London simply inviting another boy of twelve to a Christian boys' camp. That's where the younger one thanked, for the very first time, the Lord Jesus Christ for dying to pay for his sins, then simply invited Him to enter his life. A big, all-knowing God had plans for that twelve-year-old boy, who grew up to be the founder of the Torchbearer Missionary Fellowship with its conference centers and Bible schools, not only within his own country, but in many others.

From his first six years as a traveling evangelist, Ian Thomas' passion was to lead, as he so often stated, "men, women, boys and girls to Christ." This continued throughout Ian's life. In a letter from a small girl of eight or nine, now a keen Christian student at college, she wrote: "Dear Major Thomas, I enjoyed hearing you speak. Each night I took notes to count the times you said 'Jesus.' The most I counted was 73 in one night. Thank you for coming to Son Life Church."

At one time, Ian was kept in the home country for over a year, stationed in different areas of England and Scotland, involved in military exercises, he developed an attack of jaundice. Ian scribbled a small penciled note from the military hospital in Inverary, Scotland, "Are you glad you are saved this morning?" Then he wrote just four lines, which I thought were self-composed until I found on Google that they were written by a Dutchman, Gerhard Teerstegen who was born in 1697 and died in Germany in 1769. These were the brief lines that Ian sent:

> Though all the world my choice deride
> Yet Jesus shall my Portion be
> For I am pleased with none beside
> The Fairest of the Fair is He!

Hallelujah! Then the letter continued, "I am specially conscious this morning of the abundance of His grace, His mercies are new every morning and His love never fails. We are safe only so long as Christ becomes ever more precious—not the doctrine of faith, not the joys of Christian fellowship nor the privileges of service (though all these things are precious)—but

Christ Himself must be first and foremost in our hearts. May His love fill us more and more with Calvary zeal in winning lost souls to Him. Life has no value except in terms of souls saved and Christians quickened to a fuller realization and enjoyment of the spiritual 'completeness' which is to be found in Him, 'in whom dwelleth all the fullness of the Godhead bodily'" (Col. 2:9, KJV).

Students at Torchbearer Bible Schools constantly discover from God's Word the "completeness" to be found in Christ, and return home with joy in Him. While others, through Torchbearer ministries of many kinds, as lost souls find their way to Him in the small and ordinary "happenings" of the day. As Oswald Chambers writes, "We can all see God in exceptional things, but it requires the growth of spiritual discipline to see God in every detail. Never believe that the so-called random events of life are anything less than God's appointed order. Be ready to discover His divine designs anywhere and everywhere."[3]

On September 8, 1944, Ian, not yet home from war, wrote, "Have just emerged from a very blessed time of prayer and meditation, and my heart is voicing the benefits of God's salvation, but above all, the matchless wonder of the Lord Jesus Christ. I'm longing to give the old devil's tail a twist and look forward with increasing eagerness to the unshackled ministry of Life which shall be our portion when this squabble's done!"

Earlier, in May of 1944, Ian wrote to me following his experiences in the horrors of the Monte Cassino battle in Italy, since along with many other war-weary soldiers he was given leave in Bari, Italy, on the Adriatic coast and was basking in the sunshine a few yards from the sea. He wrote, "Praise the Lord! Only One Person could have brought me through unharmed and if HE did that, it has been more powerfully laid upon my heart, even these last few days, it must only be that my life, linked with yours, shall be utterly poured out for Christ and the salvation of precious souls."

So it was that I fully expected, war eventually being over, to find a little cottage in the country, while my husband continued his pre-war evangelistic ministry. Had that really happened, the story of my book would have been different. All the "little happenings" which have caused, by God's good hand, the establishment of Torchbearers with their Centres and Bible Schools around the world, would still be on God's big "drawing Board." However, as we see in First Corinthians, "God selected (deliberately chose) what in the world is foolish to put the wise to shame, and what the world calls weak to put the strong to shame. And God also selected (deliberately chose) what in the world is lowborn *and* insignificant and branded *and* treated with contempt, even the things that are nothing, that He might depose *and* bring to nothing the things that are" (1:27–28, AMP).

Why does God choose insignificant people and apparently unimportant little "happenings?" The next verse makes the reason plain, "So that no mortal man should [have pretense for glorying and] boast in the presence of God" (1:29, AMP). We can indeed reiterate, "God did it!" So, we may rejoice in our insignificance, as has been said, "Insignificant as you may seem in this great universe, you are an important part of God's plan." We are to be totally available for God and always obedient to Him.

Not only did we begin with going "just a *little* further" at the auction for Capernwray Hall in 1946, but also with a very small board meeting as recorded in a large leather-bound book kept at Capernwray Hall for the last sixty-five years. The meeting was held in Colonel Marton's old smoking room, then Ian's office and now where our son Mark directs "all over the place" and where cups of tea or coffee are the norm. The record in the old leather-bound book states that on August 4, 1947, at 9 a.m., the following first-ever board meeting was held.

Present:
> Managing Director: Major Ian Thomas
> Secretary: Major Gordon Greenwood
> Auditors: Gregsons

The business was to decide to form a limited company.

On October 2, 1947, at 11:00 a.m., Mrs. Joan Thomas was added as a director (they needed a woman), and shares were allocated to three gentlemen—good friends of ours who offered to invest in the company without anticipating any return.

That was the very small and simple beginning of the organization called Torchbearers. Just like the tiny newborn baby with little arms raised heavenwards, even those "short and very small board" meetings had the potential, while prayerfully under God's direction and guidance, to develop as He planned. Despite the mistakes and hurts that are occasionally brought about by working together under spiritual and international differences, the blessings of our great God have been beyond anything we ever asked, thought or dreamed about.

In a 1950 issue of *Torch* magazine, published at Capernwray Hall, a young German, after his spiritually fruitful visit to Capernwray, wrote the following:

> Now when I am going to write you this letter, I fear that I am unable to find the right words, but you may believe my gratitude comes from my heart when I now write, "Thank you! Thank you!" It is the expression of an indescribable feeling. It is an awful thing to see the difference between the Christians I have met in Capernwray and other places of England and the inactivity and superficiality of the

Christians of our town. It is our duty to try again and again to bring boys and girls and men and women to our Lord Jesus Christ! It is also necessary to have a *great number of Capernwrays all over the world to show people how little they use the power of the Holy Spirit!*

Always your brother in Him, Rolf

That short letter from Rolf was quoted in the very first issue of Capernwray's *Torch* magazine in which, excited and deeply grateful for all our amazing God had accomplished, we wanted all those who had been such a part of developing Torchbearers to know what God was doing. Vol. 1, No.1 of *Torch* reported the twenty letters so far received at that time from German members of the first group of young people who expressed their absolute joy at coming to know Christ for themselves.

Jürgen wrote, "I have become a completely new person in Christ." And from Johann, "I will never forget what is the most important thing—I found the Lord Jesus Christ as my Savior." Ilse wrote, "I know I am saved by grace. I am glad, glad, glad the Lord brought me to Capernwray Hall."

That was but the beginning of Torchbearers. I wonder if Rolf ever discovered that by "the power of the Holy Spirit" and using "little happenings and ordinary people," God has so far planted twenty-six Torchbearer Centres around the world.

Maybe it was a small "happening" that caused you, my reader, to pick up this book somewhere, and in reading it, discovered that you have no "torch" to bear so to bring the light and life available in Jesus Christ to others around you. Maybe you wish you could be a Torchbearer like some of those young Germans and others. The way is simple. First, like all of us, you recognize your sinful nature for which Jesus died on the cross to give you forgiveness, and for which you thank Him. Then in simple faith, you invite Him by His Holy Spirit to enter your human spirit so giving you His light and life. Jesus Himself said, "He who follows Me will not be walking in the dark but will have the Light which is Life" (John 8:12, AMP). That is why my book is about Torchbearers and how God has shown others the way to Him through them. Dear reader, you could also become a Torchbearer!

Endnotes

1. Chambers, Oswald. *My Utmost for His Highest*. (Grand Rapids, MI: Discovery House Publishers, 1992). October 24.

2. "God's Guiding Hand: Helpful Thoughts from Hudson Taylor." Quoted by permission of OMF International.

3. Chambers, Oswald. *My Utmost for His Highest*. (Grand Rapids, MI: Discovery House Publishers, 1992). November 14.

PUBLICATIONS
Fort Washington, PA 19034

This book is published by CLC Publications, an outreach of CLC Ministries International. The purpose of CLC is to make evangelical Christian literature available to all nations so that people may come to faith and maturity in the Lord Jesus Christ. We hope this book has been life changing and has enriched your walk with God through the work of the Holy Spirit. If you would like to know more about CLC, we invite you to visit our website:

www.clcusa.org

To know more about the remarkable story of the founding of CLC International we encourage you to read

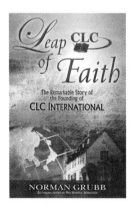

LEAP OF FAITH

Norman Grubb

Paperback
Size 5^1/$_4$ x 8, Pages 249
ISBN: 978-0-87508-650-7 - $11.99
ISBN (*e-book*): 978-1-61958-055-8 - $9.99

GETTING INTO GOD

Stuart Briscoe

Stuart Briscoe's *Getting into God* will take you through the basic elements of biblical study, prayer and witnessing. Whether you are a new Christian or one simply wanting to get back to the basics of your faith, this book offers some basic instruction on the "practicalities of Christian experience."

Paperback
Size 5¹/₄ x 8, Pages 144
ISBN: 978-1-61958-152-4 - $11.99
ISBN (*e-book*): 978-1-61958-153-1 - $9.99

RUNNING ON EMPTY

Jill Briscoe

Feeling burned out? Unfulfilled? Drained? Jill Briscoe offers hope and comfort for those times in life when we feel empty and tired. With wit and candor, Briscoe draws lessons from several biblical figures that provide spiritual refreshment and renewal to those who are *Running on Empty.*

Paperback
Size 5¹/₄ x 8, Pages 176
ISBN: 978-1-61958-080-0 - $12.99
ISBN (*e-book*): 978-1-61958-081-7 - $9.99

This book challenges us to leave casual Christianity behind and take God seriously, just as the prophets did!
Dr. Erwin W. Lutzer, Senior Pastor - The Moody Church, Chicago, IL

Taking God Seriously
Major Lessons from the Minor Prophets

Stuart Briscoe

TAKING GOD SERIOUSLY

Stuart Briscoe

Seasoned pastor Stuart Briscoe examines each of the Minor Prophets, providing both helpful historical context, and demonstrating the relevance of each prophet's message to believers today. If you want to take God's words from the Minor Prophets seriously, this book will help enrich your Bible study.

Paperback
Size 5¼ x 8, Pages 208
ISBN: 978-1-61958-078-7 - $12.99
ISBN (*e-book*): 978-1-61958-079-4 - $9.99

THE PATHWAY TO GOD'S PRESENCE

Tom Elliff

The Pathway to God's Presence encourages those who feel as though they have lost the sense of God's presence in their lives and wish greatly to restore it. Each chapter examines the Old Testament account of Moses and the often-wayward children of Israel, making clear the idea that "there is a distinct difference between God's provision and His presence."

Paperback
Size 4¹/₄ x 7, Pages 144
ISBN: 978-1-61958-156-2 - $9.99
ISBN (*e-book*): 978-1-61958-157-9 - $9.99

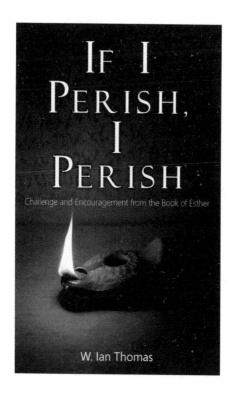

IF I PERISH, I PERISH

W. Ian Thomas

If I Perish, I Perish examines the Christian life through the lens of an allegorical interpretation of the Old Testament book of Esther. The character of Esther, representative of the human spirit, depicts that the call of the Lord Jesus on the Christian is to be crucified with Christ and become alive in the Spirit.

Paperback
Size 4 ¼ x 7, Pages 159
ISBN 978-1-61958-160-9 - $ 9.99
ISBN (*e-book*) 978-1-61958-161-6 - $9.99

GOD ON FIRE

Fred A. Hartley III

As believers, we are more alive in the middle of God's white-hot presence than anywhere else on earth. The history of revival is often studied from man's perspective; what we do to encounter God. *God on Fire* explores what God does to encounter us.

Paperback
Size 5 ¼ x 8, Pages 206
ISBN 978-1-61958-012-1 - $14.99
ISBN (*e-book*) 978-1-61958-066-4 - $9.99

LED TO LEAD

Marty Berglund

Led to Lead challenges ministry leaders to grow deeper in faith through lessons drawn from the life of Moses. This book will challenge you to learn from the life of Israel's greatest leader and to move ahead in your own life and ministry, implementing the lessons learned.

Paperback
Size 5¹/₄ x 8, Pages 256
ISBN: 978-1-61958-150-0 - $13.99
ISBN (*e-book*): 978-1-61958-151-7 - $9.99